Thompson
Book Club
2007

Regina Jackson

Purchase
Baron & Noble

What Matters Most

What Matters Most

TEN LESSONS IN LIVING PASSIONATELY FROM THE SONG OF SOLOMON

RENITA J. WEEMS

West Bloomfield, Michigan

WARNER BOOKS

NEW YORK BOSTON

With the exception of the text of the Song of Solomon that is printed here in its entirety, all quotes throughout the book are the author's translations from the original Hebrew.

Published by Warner Books. Inc., with Walk Worthy Press™

Warner Books
Time Warner Book Group
1271 Avenue of the Americas, New York, NY 10020

Walk Worthy Press
33290 West Fourteen Mile Road, # 482, West Bloomfield, MI 48322

Visit our Web sites at www.twbookmark.com and www.walkworthypress.net.

Printed in the United States of America
First Printing: April 2004
10 9 8 7 6 5 4 3 2

Library of Congress Cataloging-in-Publication Data

Weems, Renita J., 1954–
    What matters most : ten lessons in living passionately from the Song of Solomon / Renita J. Weems.
        p. cm.
    ISBN 0-446-53241-X
  1. Bible. O.T. Song of Solomon—Criticism, interpretation, etc.
2. Christian women—Religious life.   I. Title.
    BS1485.52.W44. 2004
    248.8'43—dc22

                                                        2003023051

Book design and text composition by L&G McRee

To my paternal great aunts who knew what
was important and for as long as they had strength
of body and presence of mind to do so,
they ran the family accordingly.
To paraphrase a poem by Alice Walker:

They were women then, my great aunts' generation

Annie Mag Weems (1901–1992) and
Georgian Melinda Weems Jacobs (1911–)

Contents

Song of Solomon ix

Introduction 1

The Self 13

"I have a suspicion there must be more to me than I even know."

Identity 31

"God, is that you? I didn't know."

Truth 51

"To speak up for the pleasures of love and against the injustices of life itself is to speak up for everything that God loves and represents."

Balance 65

"So why don't you get some help before you collapse?"

Choices 83
"On the basis of who you are and what you know, you must make a
decision about what path to take."

Inner Wisdom 99
"Different seasons in our lives call on different aspects of
our personality."

Danger 115
"Come what may, I will survive."

Your Body 135
"You feel it in your bones."

Sacrifice 147
"Put simply, love costs."

Sex and Love 161
"Since when did smart women begin admitting that they have
problems finding love?"

Song of Solomon

I

1 The song of songs, which *is* Solomon's.

2 Let him kiss me with the kisses of his mouth: for thy love *is* better than wine.

3 Because of the savour of thy good ointments thy name *is as* ointment poured forth, therefore do the virgins love thee.

4 Draw me, we will run after thee: the king hath brought me into his chambers: we will be glad and rejoice in thee, we will remember thy love more than wine: the upright love thee.

5 I *am* black, but comely, O ye daughters of Jerusalem, as the tents of Kedar, as the curtains of Solomon.

6 Look not upon me, because I *am* black, because the sun hath looked upon me: my mother's chil-

dren were angry with me; they made me the keeper of the vineyards; *but* mine own vineyard have I not kept.

7 Tell me, O thou whom my soul loveth, where thou feedest, where thou makest *thy flock* to rest at noon: for why should I be as one that turneth aside by the flocks of thy companions?

8 If thou know not, O thou fairest among women, go thy way forth by the footsteps of the flock, and feed thy kids beside the shepherds' tents.

9 I have compared thee, O my love, to a company of horses in Pharaoh's chariots.

10 Thy cheeks are comely with rows *of jewels*, thy neck with chains *of gold*.

11 We will make thee borders of gold with studs of silver.

12 While the king *sitteth* at his table, my spikenard sendeth forth the smell thereof.

13 A bundle of myrrh *is* my well-beloved unto me; he shall lie all night betwixt my breasts.

14 My beloved *is* unto me *as* a cluster of camphire in the vineyards of Engedi.

15 Behold, thou *art* fair, my love; behold, thou *art* fair; thou *hast* doves' eyes.

16 Behold, thou *art* fair, my beloved, yea, pleasant: also our bed *is* green.

17 The beams of our house *are* cedar, *and* our rafters of fir.

II

1 I *am* the rose of Sharon, *and* the lily of the valleys.

2 As the lily among thorns, so *is* my love among the daughters.

3 As the apple tree among the trees of the wood, so *is* my beloved among the sons. I sat down under his shadow with great delight, and his fruit *was* sweet to my taste.

4 He brought me to the banqueting house, and his banner over me *was* love.

5 Stay me with flagons, comfort me with apples: for I *am* sick of love.

6 His left hand *is* under my head, and his right hand doth embrace me.

7 I charge you, O ye daughters of Jerusalem, by the roes, and by the hinds of the field, that ye stir not up, nor awake *my* love, till he please.

8 The voice of my beloved! behold, he cometh leaping upon the mountains, skipping upon the hills.

9 My beloved is like a roe or a young hart: behold, he standeth behind our wall, he looketh forth at the windows, shewing himself through the lattice.

10 My beloved spake, and said unto me, Rise up, my love, my fair one, and come away.

11 For, lo, the winter is past, the rain is over *and* gone;

12 The flowers appear on the earth; the time of the singing *of birds* is come, and the voice of the turtle is heard in our land;

13 The fig tree putteth forth her green figs, and the vines *with* the tender grape give a *good* smell. Arise, my love, my fair one, and come away.

14 O my dove, *that art* in the clefts of the rock, in the secret *places* of the stairs, let me see thy countenance, let me hear thy voice; for sweet *is* thy voice, and thy countenance *is* comely.

15 Take us the foxes, the little foxes, that spoil the vines: for our vines *have* tender grapes.

16 My beloved *is* mine, and I *am* his: he feedeth among the lilies.

17 Until the day break, and the shadows flee away, turn, my beloved, and be thou like a roe or a young hart upon the mountains of Bether.

III

1 By night on my bed I sought him whom my soul loveth: I sought him, but I found him not.

2 I will rise now, and go about the city in the streets, and in the broad ways I will seek him whom my soul loveth: I sought him, but I found him not.

3 The watchmen that go about the city found me: *to whom I said*, Saw ye him whom my soul loveth?

4 *It was* but a little that I passed from them, but I found him whom my soul loveth: I held him, and would

not let him go, until I had brought him into my mother's house, and into the chamber of her that conceived me.

5 I charge you, O ye daughters of Jerusalem, by the roes, and by the hinds of the field, that ye stir not up, nor awake *my* love, till he please.

6 Who *is* this that cometh out of the wilderness like pillars of smoke, perfumed with myrrh and frankincense, with all powders of the merchant?

7 Behold his bed, which *is* Solomon's; threescore valiant men *are* about it, of the valiant of Israel.

8 They all hold swords, *being* expert in war: every man *hath* his sword upon his thigh because of fear in the night.

9 King Solomon made himself a chariot of the wood of Lebanon.

10 He made the pillars thereof *of* silver, the bottom thereof *of* gold, the covering of it *of* purple, the midst thereof being paved *with* love, for the daughters of Jerusalem.

11 Go forth, O ye daughters of Zion, and behold king Solomon with the crown wherewith his mother crowned him in the day of his espousals, and in the day of the gladness of his heart.

IV

1 Behold, thou *art* fair, my love; behold, thou *art* fair; thou *hast* doves' eyes within thy locks: thy hair

is as a flock of goats, that appear from mount Gilead.

2 Thy teeth *are* like a flock of *sheep* that are *even* shorn, which came up from the washing; whereof every one bear twins, and none *is* barren among them.

3 Thy lips *are* like a thread of scarlet, and thy speech *is* comely: thy temples *are* like a piece of a pomegranate within thy locks.

4 Thy neck *is* like the tower of David builded for an armoury, whereon there hang a thousand bucklers, all shields of mighty men.

5 Thy two breasts *are* like two young roes that are twins, which feed among the lilies.

6 Until the day break, and the shadows flee away, I will get me to the mountain of myrrh, and to the hill of frankincense.

7 Thou *art* all fair, my love; *there is* no spot in thee.

8 Come with me from Lebanon, *my* spouse, with me from Lebanon: look from the top of Amana, from the top of Shenir and Hermon, from the lions' dens, from the mountains of the leopards.

9 Thou hast ravished my heart, my sister, *my* spouse; thou hast ravished my heart with one of thine eyes, with one chain of thy neck.

10 How fair is thy love, my sister, *my* spouse! how much better is thy love than wine! and the smell of thine ointments than all spices!

11 Thy lips, O *my* spouse, drop *as* the honeycomb: honey and milk *are* under thy tongue; and the smell of thy garments *is* like the smell of Lebanon.

12 A garden enclosed *is* my sister, *my* spouse; a spring shut up, a fountain sealed.

13 Thy plants *are* an orchard of pomegranates, with pleasant fruits; camphire, with spikenard,

14 Spikenard and saffron; calamus and cinnamon, with all trees of frankincense; myrrh and aloes, with all the chief spices:

15 A fountain of gardens, a well of living waters, and streams from Lebanon.

16 Awake, O north wind; and come, thou south; blow upon my garden, *that* the spices thereof may flow out. Let my beloved come into his garden, and eat his pleasant fruits.

V

1 I am come into my garden, my sister, *my* spouse: I have gathered my myrrh with my spice; I have eaten my honeycomb with my honey; I have drunk my wine with my milk: eat, O friends; drink, yea, drink abundantly, O beloved.

2 I sleep, but my heart waketh: *it is* the voice of my beloved that knocketh, *saying*, Open to me, my sister, my love, my dove, my undefiled: for my head is filled with dew, *and* my locks with the drops of the night.

3 I have put off my coat; how shall I put it on? I have washed my feet; how shall I defile them?

4 My beloved put in his hand by the hole *of the door*, and my bowels were moved for him.

5 I rose up to open to my beloved; and my hands dropped *with* myrrh, and my fingers *with* sweet-smelling myrrh, upon the handles of the lock.

6 I opened to my beloved; but my beloved had withdrawn himself, *and* was gone: my soul failed when he spake: I sought him, but I could not find him; I called him, but he gave me no answer.

7 The watchmen that went about the city found me, they smote me, they wounded me; the keepers of the walls took away my veil from me.

8 I charge you, O daughters of Jerusalem, if ye find my beloved, that ye tell him, that I *am* sick of love.

9 What *is* thy beloved more than *another* beloved, O thou fairest among women? what *is* thy beloved more than *another* beloved, that thou dost so charge us?

10 My beloved *is* white and ruddy, the chiefest among ten thousand.

11 His head *is as* the most fine gold, his locks *are* bushy, *and* black as a raven.

12 His eyes *are* as *the eyes* of doves by the rivers of waters, washed with milk, *and* fitly set.

13 His cheeks *are* as a bed of spices, *as* sweet flowers: his lips *like* lilies, dropping sweet-smelling myrrh.

14 His hands *are as* gold rings set with the beryl: his belly *is as* bright ivory overlaid *with* sapphires.

15 His legs *are as* pillars of marble, set upon sockets of fine gold: his countenance *is* as Lebanon, excellent as the cedars.

16 His mouth *is* most sweet: yea, he *is* altogether lovely. This *is* my beloved, and this *is* my friend, O daughters of Jerusalem.

VI

1 Whither is thy beloved gone, O thou fairest among women? whither is thy beloved turned aside? that we may seek him with thee.

2 My beloved is gone down into his garden, to the beds of spices, to feed in the gardens, and to gather lilies.

3 I *am* my beloved's, and my beloved *is* mine: he feedeth among the lilies.

4 Thou *art* beautiful, O my love, as Tirzah, comely as Jerusalem, terrible as *an army* with banners.

5 Turn away thine eyes from me, for they have overcome me: thy hair *is* as a flock of goats that appear from Gilead.

6 Thy teeth *are* as a flock of sheep which go up from the washing, whereof every one beareth twins, and *there is* not one barren among them.

7 As a piece of a pomegranate *are* thy temples within thy locks.

8 There are threescore queens, and fourscore concubines, and virgins without number.

9 My dove, my undefiled is *but* one; she *is* the *only*
one of her mother, she *is* the choice *one* of her that
bare her. The daughters saw her, and blessed her;
yea, the queens and the concubines, and they
praised her.

10 Who *is* she *that* looketh forth as the morning, fair
as the moon, clear as the sun, *and* terrible as *an
army* with banners?

11 I went down into the garden of nuts to see the fruits
of the valley, *and* to see whether the vine flourished,
and the pomegranates budded.

12 Or ever I was aware, my soul made me *like* the
chariots of Amminadib.

13 Return, return, O Shulamite; return, return, that
we may look upon thee. What will ye see in the
Shulamite? As it were the company of two
armies.

VII

1 How beautiful are thy feet with shoes, O prince's
daughter! the joints of thy thighs *are* like jewels,
the work of the hands of a cunning work-
man.

2 Thy navel *is like* a round goblet, *which* wanteth not
liquor: thy belly *is like* an heap of wheat set about
with lilies.

3 Thy two breasts *are* like two young roes *that are* twins.

4 Thy neck *is* as a tower of ivory; thine eyes *like* the fishpools in Heshbon, by the gate of Bathrabbim: thy nose *is* as the tower of Lebanon which looketh toward Damascus.

5 Thine head upon thee *is* like Carmel, and the hair of thine head like purple; the king *is* held in the galleries.

6 How fair and how pleasant art thou, O love, for delights!

7 This thy stature is like to a palm tree, and thy breasts to clusters of *grapes*.

8 I said, I will go up to the palm tree, I will take hold of the boughs thereof: now also thy breasts shall be as clusters of the vine, and the smell of thy nose like apples;

9 And the roof of thy mouth like the best wine for my beloved, that goeth *down* sweetly, causing the lips of those that are asleep to speak.

10 I *am* my beloved's, and his desire *is* toward me.

11 Come, my beloved, let us go forth into the field; let us lodge in the villages.

12 Let us get up early to the vineyards; let us see if the vine flourish, *whether* the tender grape appear, *and* the pomegranates bud forth: there will I give thee my loves.

13 The mandrakes give a smell, and at our gates *are*

all manner of pleasant *fruits*, new and old, *which* I have laid up for thee, O my beloved.

VIII

1 O that thou *wert* as my brother, that sucked the breasts of my mother! *when* I should find thee without, I would kiss thee; yea, I should not be despised.

2 I would lead thee, *and* bring thee into my mother's house, *who* would instruct me: I would cause thee to drink of spiced wine of the juice of my pomegranate.

3 His left hand *should be* under my head, and his right hand should embrace me.

4 I charge you, O daughters of Jerusalem, that ye stir not up, nor awake *my* love, until he please.

5 Who *is* this that cometh up from the wilderness, leaning upon her beloved? I raised thee up under the apple tree: there thy mother brought thee forth: there she brought thee forth *that* bare thee.

6 Set me as a seal upon thine heart, as a seal upon thine arm: for love *is* strong as death; jealousy *is* cruel as the grave: the coals thereof *are* coals of fire, *which hath a* most vehement flame.

7 Many waters cannot quench love, neither can the floods drown it: if a man would give all the substance of his house for love, it would utterly be contemned.

8 We have a little sister, and she hath no breasts: what shall we do for our sister in the day when she shall be spoken for?

9 If she *be* a wall, we will build upon her a palace of silver: and if she *be* a door, we will inclose her with boards of cedar.

10 I *am* a wall, and my breasts like towers: then was I in his eyes as one that found favour.

11 Solomon had a vineyard at Baal-hamon; he let out the vineyard unto keepers; every one for the fruit thereof was to bring a thousand *pieces* of silver.

12 My vineyard, which *is* mine, *is* before me: thou, O Solomon, *must have* a thousand, and those that keep the fruit thereof two hundred.

13 Thou that dwellest in the gardens, the companions hearken to thy voice: cause me to hear *it*.

14 Make haste, my beloved, and be thou like to a roe or to a young hart upon the mountains of spices.

(KJV)

What Matters Most

Introduction

"What if I am the one responsible for going after the life I've spent my whole life praying for?" The question caught me off guard. The woman standing before me had chosen not to say very much in class over the past seven weeks, and now it was taking me a moment to get accustomed to the sound of a voice coming from her body. "After spending years of waiting to be rescued, waiting to find happiness, waiting to be loved, and praying that someone or something outside myself would see my predicament and answer my prayers, are you saying that it's up to me?" "*What if* . . . is the question every woman eventually has to ask herself," I replied, looking straight into the eyes of this fortyish-looking woman who'd kept her eyes down and glued to the pages of a worn Bible she'd kept open and atop her desk every week of class. It was difficult to know whether the pinched expression on her face this evening was because of her hairstyle or the discussion that had just taken place in class on the headstrong, passionate woman in Song of Solomon. We stood for a moment staring at each other. I feared saying more. I didn't want to risk bruising the candlewick trying to catch afire inside her. Sometimes it's not the right answers that we need, but the right questions to catch hold and stir us. *"What if I am the one I've been waiting for all these years?"*

We walked out of the classroom together, parted in the parking lot without another word spoken between us, and drove off in different directions. The woman with the pinched face didn't show up the next week for the last class. But then she didn't have to. She'd passed the class by coming up with the right question.

You can learn a lot from a woman who follows her own instincts and desires. Examine her life closely, and you're apt to discover that one reason she follows her own compass is a lingering suspicion on her part that she alone is responsible for securing her future and for making herself happy. You might not expect to find in the Bible a tale about a woman who takes responsibility for her own happiness. But her commitment to life, love, and learning makes the unnamed woman in Song of Solomon a ripe example of what a woman bent upon forging a life for herself might look like. She is headstrong, passionate, gutsy, and willing to risk the disapproval of those around her in order to pursue her own happiness. The feisty, unnamed woman in Song of

Solomon is every woman who prays to God for a soul-satisfying life, only to turn around and find God forcing her into situations where she must come to grips with her role in making her prayers a reality.

It's a shame that we don't have a proper name for this woman who appears as one of the most stubbornly self-possessed women in Scripture. Like so many women in the Bible, she steps onto its pages anonymous and nameless. Anyone, however, who leaves cautionary lessons from her own story behind for those coming after her deserves to be properly memorialized. But like lots of women in the Bible, a full biographical portrait of the woman behind the poetry in Song of Solomon is off-limits to us. Twice in 6:13 she is referred to "the Shulammite," which probably tells us more about the village in which she was born—a village scholars speculate was called Shulem—than it does about the woman she was. In this regard, she was like Mary from the village of Magdala, dubbed "the Magdalene," although we know next to nothing about either woman's background or origin. But in the eight chapters and 117 verses that contain her life's dreams known as Song of Solomon, she rises from the pages as a force to be reckoned with. By whispering her secrets and sharing her fantasies as a woman, she upstages the men in the Bible, who frequently get top billing. Her poems to her unnamed lover have a way of sneaking into the bloodstream and making you think out loud about your own complicated, unexamined desires. By fantasizing openly about intimacy with her shepherd lover and about stealing away for some erotic rendezvous with him, she forces us to confront head-on our deepest convictions, our unspoken preconceptions, and our own complicated wishes. Being sexual is part of being human, her poems remind us.

This puzzling little book, known as Song of Solomon, or as Song of Songs or as Canticles, is composed of love poetry that is quite frankly erotic. The woman's open, candid talk about love, passion, desire, and longing reminds us that we are not just spiritual and rational creatures. We are indisputably physical and sexual beings, despite all of our Sunday morning, high and holy pretentions. Her poetry, which continues to baffle scholars, commentators, Christian and Jewish inter-preters, and ordinary readers alike, refuses to conform itself to our notions of religious respectability. It refuses to let its steamy tale of desire and lust be explained away, however exaltedly, as metaphor for our religious longings. Sexuality is as old as creation itself, it insists. In fact, the sexual part of our humanity is as strong as death and as unquenchable as fire. That is because sex is frequently the drama around which we attempt des-perately to capture our deepest desires, our most feverish longings, our recurring dreams, and our most aching loneliness.

By following our heroine's fantasies and courtship with a certain unnamed shepherd-lover, observing the obstacles she encounters in her culture and those she must face from within, we witness her growing and developing as she faces one hurdle after another and keeps moving forward. Reared in a culture that barred women from the public world of work and politics, a world that considered family, home, and romance as the proper spheres for women's dreams and passions, the Shulammite shows us the lessons a woman learns and unlearns a hundred times when she sets out to discover what passion truly entails. Passion is not something you find; it's a part of who you are already. It's not just for sex and romance; passion is what you pour into creating a life for yourself that has meaning and purpose.

The Shulammite's story is one we know by heart as women. She falls in love and invests all her hopes, dreams, and passions in a relationship that never pans out to be what she imagined. It's a romance, quite frankly, that eludes both her and her readers from beginning to end. Her affair with the skittish shepherd-lover can never be pinned down exactly. From the book's opening to its close, her beloved refuses to stay put, refuses to reveal himself, refuses to step out from behind the bushes to be seen. It's the story of the forever absent lover. The furtive lover. The secret love affair. The doomed date. The exasperating courtship. The shepherd is the sweetheart you cling to but never quite possess. The courtship that looks better on paper than in reality. The fantasy that was sweeter than the actual rendezvous. Song of Solomon is a book about fantasies, a woman's fantasies, the ones that lead us to unexpected discoveries about ourselves. Also the ones that don't quite turn out as we expected, and thank God they didn't. We might have given ourselves completely away.

You start out believing in the promises of romance, investing lots of your energy and passions into finding love and/or keeping some semblance of it in your life, hoping that love and sexual desire will rescue you and deliver you from the tedium of existence. But they don't. Eventually, you have to face the reality that while love and romance can (and often do) enrich life, they don't save you from having to grow up and face a self who has her own purpose for being. Our heroine teaches us the *real* lessons of living passionately, of not fearing our passions and not allowing them to be exploited, tapping into them to find our strengths and a new realm of spiritual intimacy with God, trusting them to open up new experiences for us and to point us to the people, places, and things that really matter. By peeling back the layers of the Shulammite's poetic journey, we come face to face with a woman rooted in wholehearted involvements, a woman in Scripture bent on living a meaningful life, however unconventional it may have seemed to others.

It takes a bold, gutsy, free-spirited woman to strike out on her own journey to discover what's important to her and to claim what's important for herself. Hence, the title of the book, *What Matters Most*, reminds us of the juicy, outrageous Shulammite in all of us who is prepared to make choices and take risks to live a life ignited by our own inner flame. Our heroine beckons us back to our first love, our desire to live a full and fulfilling life based on those things dear to us. It is fitting that her story is mediated through the lush, evocative, playful guise of lyrical poetry. Lyrical poems cast as passionate dialogues, erotic soliloquies, and private dreams function in Song of Solomon as the discourse of interior life and the rhetoric of heartfelt emotions. Hardly anything written in classical secular romance literature can match the exquisitely provocative exchanges between the anonymous female protagonist and her shepherd suitor in Song of Solomon.

Love poetry was prominent throughout the ancient Near East, and although most written accounts that still exist today can be traced back to the Egyptian and Mesopotamian civilizations, Song of Solomon stands out in contrast to other love poems, which are typically monologues, in its use of love poetry as a form of dialogue between the two lovers, dialogue between the Shulammite and her Jerusalem girlfriends, dialogue between the Shulammite and her own self. As for its contrast with the rest of the Bible, Song of Solomon stands out in two important ways. First, nowhere in its eight chapters is God mentioned, which gives the book a decidedly secular tone. (Esther is the only other book in the Bible that shares this distinction.) The Shulammite's failure to mention God wasn't due to any irreverence on her part, but was more likely the consequence of her effort not to appeal to God to rationalize her fears or to justify the side of her that longed for someone to come along and rescue her from herself.

The Shulammite's passionate, sometimes racy lyrics in Song of Solomon allow us into her conversations with herself, her beloved, her culture, her brothers, her friends the "daughters of Jerusalem," and even God about why giving yourself away to make others' dreams come true is not enough. Her poems attest to the battle she waged not so much with God, but with herself and those around her to reclaim herself. The motive behind penning love poetry such as this remains uncertain. But most commentators believe that ancient love poems were written strictly for entertainment purposes. Some believe that they were sung at festivities and banquets. Although God is sometimes referred to in many poems as an embodiment of intense or "divine" emotion between lovers, religion played an important role in these poems because it is often on religious occasions that lovers in these poems first meet.

The second way in which Song of Solomon stands out is that it is the only book in the Bible in which a woman's voice predominates from beginning to end. It is a wonderful book to help us reconnect with our own passions as women, hurling us as it does in its opening verses straight into the clutches of a headstrong woman who is determined to get from life what she feels is hers to have. Nowhere else in Scripture is so much attention paid to the desires and fantasies of a headstrong, unconventional woman. Her poems have been neatly packaged under Solomon's name, which have led scholars for centuries to debate over the book's origins, but there's no denying that dominant female voice, and strong female imagery lends the book the semblance of meditations from a woman's heart. To read the poetry of this woman, who by her own admission was a black-skinned woman (1:5), is to be reminded by a wise woman that there are turning points in our lives when we are called upon to make decisions. We have to decide what and how much we are willing to risk to create for ourselves the lives we dream and pray about. We have to decide whether we're going to stay true to ourselves and come up with ways to do just that, or we're going to give away bits and pieces of ourselves for the sake of peace, convention, relationships, and reputation. There are those critical life moments when how we choose is tied up with who we will become.

"We do not remember days," wrote the Italian novelist and poet Cesare Pavese, "we remember moments." *What Matters Most* connects us with what I have identified as the ten *nodal points*, to use a term coined by psychiatrist Jean Shinoda Bolen. These are decision-making moments in a woman's life that nudge her to become more awake than before and that invite her on a path to become a different woman than she was before, or is now. There are those moments in your life when you find yourself called upon to decide on something, between some things, about somebody, and somewhere deep inside, you know that this decision will cost you. It's a forever kind of decision. You have to decide, and the consequence of the decision will affect who *you* will be after this moment. This decision will not just change your circumstance; it will permanently alter *you*.

Decisions about love, security, relationships, career, health, family, finances, faith thrust themselves upon our consciousness innumerable times throughout our lives, but haven't you noticed those times when some decisions *feel* different. Thousands of small and large decisions are made in a lifetime, but there are the ones that rise up and catch you by the throat. They scream at you to pay attention. Listen within. What is your heart telling you? You're at a critical intersection in your life, a fork in the road, a shift inside. The planets have lined up; heaven is holding its breath; ancestors are peering over your shoulder; you are staring back at yourself. These are the decisions that touch the essence of you, that make you face up to certain things: What do you want out of your life, how do you feel about yourself, what do you believe about yourself, how much truth can you stand, where do you feel the spirit leading you, what choices are you willing to make in order to become her, and what sacrifices are you willing to make to go *there?* Choose. Decide. Risk. Dare. Who will you be? What matters most? No one ever tells us that it's precisely these moments (designed often by God) that help us discover who we are inside. They test us, they refine us, they make us, they break us, and then they leave us strong in our broken places. We are forever changed once we face these moments and choose which path we will take.

Use the pages of *What Matters Most* to connect with

your deepest desires. What do you do that makes you lose yourself and all sense of time because it nourishes and revitalizes you? If you can't say for sure what that is, then that's all the more reason why you must take your time with *What Matters Most*. I invite you to connect with your passions and discover your secret longings as you learn more about Song of Solomon and the feisty Shulammite who is its protagonist. Imagine yourself as the Shulammite. Use the margins of the pages here to write about your discoveries. Think out loud, scribble down your reactions, talk back to the Shulammite, revisit your own journey, and think back to those pivotal moments in your life when you found yourself called upon to choose between who you were and who you wanted to become. How did you choose? What do you know now that you wish you'd known back then? Tap into your dreams by writing down whatever you are feeling, fearing, hoping, or praying. Get it on the page. Read a few pages a day, if that suits you. Invite others to join you as part of a book circle as a way to get more acquainted with the Shulammite in Song of Solomon. Compare notes.

Finally, *What Matters Most* attempts to capture the rendezvous with desire that our heroine embarks upon as a way of inviting us as modern readers to contemplate all the journeys we've taken, both romantic and spiritual, both fulfilling and dead-end, and the ones yet to be taken, where you started off thinking that you wanted one thing, only to discover halfway through the journey that it was really something else (*also*) that you were after. The one thing you learn for sure is that with the journey come lessons, things to be learned, musings to be mastered, and insights to be awakened that force you to grow, mature, and become a new and better self, a more spiritually alive self. Our inspiration is the Shulammite in Song of Solomon because she teaches us to live life with courage and passion.

Could it be that the reason so many of us are unable to name our own passions is that we've never stopped long enough to notice or nurture what stirs our own psyches? We've so exhausted ourselves by fanning everyone else's flame, and called that our passion, that we never bothered noticing the embers left untended within. What we're sorely missing most in our own lives is an inner source of energy that is powerful enough to make us face ourselves. When we allow that energy to flow into all areas of our lives, it infuses each experience, every encounter, each life-changing moment with vitality, magic, and meaning.

The Self

❧

*"I have a suspicion there must be more to me
than I even know."*

Your desire for a full and fulfilling life begins with
your resisting the definitions and labels others place on
you to define who you are and their attempt to tell you
what you ought to want. The moment comes when you
have to decide for yourself who you are and what your
own desires and fantasies are. You also have to figure out
what it will take to turn your fantasies into reality and
whether you've got what it takes.

If defining who you are, knowing where you end and
where others begin, and figuring out a way to find the
time and energy to accomplish the goals you've set out
for yourself sound impossible to you, then beware of
giving yourself away to love. Falling in love, as exhila-
rating as it feels in the beginning, can cost a woman large
chunks of herself if she isn't attentive to its snares. In the

male-dominated world in which the Shulammite lived, women were raised to believe that they had to acquiesce in order to be loved; men were raised to believe that to love was to possess, control, and know better than those they love what was best for them. Such thinking still lingers in our modern society. The tragedy in our upbringing is that men have been allowed to mistake our caring for them as proof of our inherent weakness and our wish for harmony as evidence of our submission. Conversely, women have been raised to mistake domination for love and lust for intimacy. Blending your heart and hopes with another and negotiating your way through a land mine of assumptions and expectations while bartering to keep a piece of you that you recognize takes pit bull tenacity. Who has that much energy? Most women don't, in light of all the other obligations they are juggling. Small wonder that many acquiesce to the pressure to give in and give up on their own passions in order to achieve "harmony."

Odd, isn't it? A man falls in love and everyone cranes to see the woman who has agreed to soften his edges. His status does not change, not substantially anyway. He remains his own man, or is certainly expected to do so. A woman falls in love, however, and both her image and status change. She goes from "Miss" to "Mrs.," and folks immediately begin to defer to the man to whom she is attached. She is no longer "Shula the Shulammite," but "Mrs. Solomon," or the woman who has been seen cavorting around town with Solomon. Whatever dreams and desires she had of her own are expected to be neatly folded into her husband's ambitions once she marries or falls in love. Attention shifts from her dreams to his dreams. She is expected to gladly redirect whatever passions she once poured into her ambitions, her hobbies, and her career, and throw herself into helping him become the man he dreams of becoming. Love adds to his possibilities for the future because he has a wife to help him get where he's going, whereas it can turn a woman into an appendage or, more likely, someone's property if she's not careful.

You would think, for example, that it's a common enough practice for a married woman to retain her last name that no one would bother to look up when my husband and I introduce ourselves by our own given last name, his last name being one thing and mine being another. But it isn't so. The woman at the laundry where I've taken my clothes for fourteen years still shakes her head when I correct her and remind her that my last name is not that of my husband. Even worse, friends who've known me for twenty-five years, who've met my husband only once, and only briefly, insist upon introducing me by my husband's name even though they've never heard me refer to myself as anything other than "Renita Weems." Recall the outrage expressed in the media when a certain Hillary Rodham Clinton insisted upon retaining "Rodham" as part of her official name.

It's no wonder then that the book containing the Shulammite's poem is called "The Song of Solomon." Look closely and you'll notice that the book's title all but turns the Shulammite into someone other than who she was. The superscription to the book (literally translated as "The Song of Songs, which is Solomon's") gives the impression that King Solomon had something to do with the sensual poems found within. Probably appended to the book by a later editor, the book's title threatens to overshadow the value of the Shulammite's poetry. She was not one of the lovesick women in Solomon's harem. But that's who later audiences thought of when they stumbled across her steamy poetry. In fact, from medieval times until not that long ago it was universally believed that not only is Solomon the one the poet is in a froth over, but that the Queen of Sheba of 2 Kings 11 is the lusty woman who first whispered the poems in Solomon's ear upon meeting him sometime around 950 BCE. Why the Queen of Sheba? Ancient interpreters saw in the poet's self-assertion, "I am black and beautiful . . . ," an indication that the woman was from a faraway land, like the Queen of Sheba, somewhere like Arabia or Africa. In fact, a long history of ancient artwork and writings pair Solomon and Sheba together as lovers, seeing in the poetry of Song of Solomon a testimony of a steamy love affair that went on between the two. Imagine the Queen of Sheba leaning over and whispering in Solomon's ear:

> Set me as a seal upon your heart,
> as a seal upon your arm
> For love is stronger than Death,

Passion more relentless than Sheol.
Its arrows are of fire, a mighty flame ablaze.
Mighty waters cannot quench Love,
nor can torrents sweep it away.
If one offered all his wealth for love,
he would be laughed to scorn . . .

(8:6–7)

The belief has been that any woman bold enough to confess her red-hot passion had to be someone along the lines of the hundreds of women King Solomon, according to legend, kept in his harem (I Kings 11:1–8). The king's reputation as a Casanova among women, bedmate as he was to seven hundred wives and three hundred concubines, made him a popular subject of folk tales and folk music. No doubt, plenty of speculation and tales arose about the kind of women who fell for men like Solomon. Gullible. Needy. Desperate. Weak. Loose. A stalker. Any woman bold enough to talk openly about her passion in polite company, like the Shulammite, had to be a harlot. If not a harlot, then she was certainly the kind of woman who falls prey to philanderers and gigolos. She was a goner. A floozy. Another strike against our heroine is the fact that there's no explicit mention besides one oblique reference (about Solomon's wedding day) in 3:11 to marriage and marrying. There's no indication that the Shulammite and her lover are married to each other or to other people. Wow!! Eight chapters teeming with lust, love, sex, and passion in the middle of the Bible—and not once does the heroine or her beloved talk about marriage as a way to seal their love and as the institution in which they might properly express their pent-up sexual frustration. Is the book a pamphlet in the Bible that condones sex outside of marriage? I doubt it.

There's sure to be those reading *What Matters Most* who will take great exception to my choice to concentrate on a literal rather than figurative reading of the contents of Song of Solomon. Why not follow the Church's lead and read the book's contents as a spiritual allegory where the dark headstrong woman and shepherd lover transform into Israel and God, or the Church and Christ. That way we can safely dispense with the Song's racy sexual overtones. Reading the book as an allegory, a pictorial representation of an otherwise abstract or lofty teaching, is the way generations of interpreters have scrambled to explain how the book made its way into the Bible. But the truth is that those who sat down and decided which books would make the cut into the Bible and which ones should be tossed did not bother to leave any guidelines to help us understand the standards they applied. None of us knows for sure what they had in mind when they voted in favor of a book like Song of Solomon, which doesn't even bother to mention God by name. The fact that the book traces its inspiration back to one of Israel's wisest and most revered kings, Solomon, no doubt was a factor in their decision.

One thing for certain is those who championed Song of Solomon's inclusion must be admired. They worked overtime to persuade the stuffy officials deciding such things in their day of the similarities between erotic desire and a healthy spirituality. The notion that an erotic passion is akin in some important ways to spiritual anticipation was an idea whose time had come. Marrying off the lovers would permanently alter their lust and make it ill suited to capturing the longing that fuels the spiritual journey. The notion that love is a form of death—death to a former self and death to a certain way of being in the world—was irresistibly reasonable to those who pondered the argument. You can never return to your former self once you've loved. The funny thing about romance is that it awakens you to fresh realities and simultaneously dulls you to some others.

For years I was admittedly reluctant to devote any research to the lovestruck woman in Song of Solomon. The image of a love-starved woman pining away for romance was the exact opposite of what I felt contemporary women should draw inspiration from. The media has seen to it that there is no shortage of sexually provocative bimbo female characters to draw from television sitcoms. Why add to the harem of images of love-starved women that are popular in our culture, I reasoned. Excavating the life of a woman in Scripture who potentially fed into popular notions of women as "dolls, babes, and bimbos" was not the way I wanted to spend my passions.

I'm willing to admit now that my prejudices against the woman in Song of Solomon were fueled somewhat by my own ambivalence about love and identity. I admit now that I was guilty of doing the very thing I've been arguing throughout the chapter not to do. I was looking at the Shulammite through the eyes of everyone else (ancient interpreters and contemporary pundits). I hadn't bothered trying to see her through her own eyes and testimony. I was dismissing a woman's genuine search for intimacy as simply a pathetic story about trying to get laid. The social and theological value of her testimony completely escaped me. It took me some time to appreciate that, unlike so many other stories in the Bible centering around the male search for self, the Shulammite was not extolling solitude, individuality, separation, and aloneness as the sole path for encountering God. Our poet doesn't hurl laws and oracles at us to shame us for our wanting affection and our craving to be touched. She identifies with her readers by tapping into our desire for intimacy, crooning about our desire for experiences that take us outside ourselves, and reminding us of our need to be connected. Hers is a story about a woman who discovers God and herself *not* through abandoning her family (as did the disciples of Jesus), or refraining from marriage (as did many of the prophets of Israel), or withdrawing for extended periods of prayer and exceptional study (as did Elijah, Huldah, Paul, and others). Everything she discovers about God and herself she learns from the messy lessons that come with risking intimacy: the nicks and bruises that come with living in the shaky bonds of mutuality and love; and the egg that cracks over your head whenever you set out trying to have a love life and make a name for yourself at the same time.

When the time came to sit down and write this, my fifth book on women's spiritual growth and inner wisdom, I had in mind every woman I'd ever encountered who drew a blank when asked to describe what she felt passionate enough about to risk things precious to her in order to pursue it. I thought about every woman who answered honestly in saying, "I don't know what my passions are." There were also those who couldn't bring themselves to admit they didn't know and tried gallantly to name things that ignited them. Most ended up pointing to the amount of time and energy they poured into their families, the effort they put into their friendships, and the long hours they devoted to work as evidence of their commitments. But there's a difference between the life energy we devote to sustaining other people's dreams, and the life energy we invest in keeping our own soul alive and stimulated. As one woman aptly put it after her family, friends, and work list was completed, "I love my life and all the people in it, but I have a suspicion there must be more to me than I even know." She's right. There is more to all of us than even we know.

Falling in love awakens something in a woman that's nearly impossible to put back to sleep once it's been roused. It has a similar effect on girls, which is why a teenage daughter in love sends a mother into hysterics. Which probably explains why the poet cautions, "I adjure you daughters of Jerusalem that you do not awaken love until it's time" (2:7; 3:5; 8:4). Love, even the pretense of it, can reduce a confident, self-assured woman who runs a department of employees to a babbling indecisive girl. Compare the strong, confident woman in Song of Solomon 1:5–7 who knows who she is and what she wants to the simpering, heartsick figure in 5:2–6 who can't decide whether to answer his knock or not, go after him when he leaves her or not. If love can make oatmeal of a woman with experience under her belt, imagine what it can do to a young girl who lacks the spiritual muscle it takes to bear up under its vicissitudes. It can leave a young girl tearing her hair and heart out when she hasn't enough experience to know how to negotiate its demands nor to know her true worth.

When you're fifteen, a romantic breakup feels irrecoverable. You tell yourself that you won't survive the heartbreak and that nothing else could possibly be worse than the awful pain you're in right now. At thirty-five, you know you'll survive this breakup, although a part of you doesn't want to because nothing will make you happier than to make him hurt as bad as you're hurting right now, even though you know better. Still you wonder whether he knows how much pain you're in right now and imagine summoning the courage to go to his place, knock on his door, then hurl every item he ever bought you in his face and storm away. But you know better, and wonder how long you can cling to the possibility that he'll come to his senses and come back to you before you feel like an idiot even to yourself. At fifty, you collapse to the floor in sobs when he decides that you're not the one he wants to spend the second half of his life with. You wail. You puke. You curse him for reducing you to feeling like a simpering teenager. You talk yourself out of begging. You can't return to the giddy, awestruck, acquiescent maiden you once were to satisfy him. Eventually you dry your eyes, reapply your makeup, and decide that surviving and going on with your life are the best revenge.

Listening to the Shulammite pour out her heart to the shepherd, one begins to understand how easy it is to dismiss her as a lovesick woman who needn't be taken seriously. Indeed, the lyrics she uses to describe her longing belong to a whole tradition of aching songs women have sung down through the years about men they were better off not loving. Let's call them "heartbreak songs," those "I love you, but I wish I didn't love you" songs. They are songs to acquaintances, lovers, husbands, or other women's husbands begging them to stay, do right, come back, or release the woman so she can go on with her life. For a period there the Shulammite is caught between a rock and a hard place. She loves her beloved shepherd. She pines for him. She dreams of him. And he loves her (she thinks; she hopes). But the romance can't be consummated; things just never come together. I am reminded of a whole jukebox of achy songs that have accompanied me through every romance I've experienced: "I Never Loved a Man the Way I Love You," by

Aretha Franklin. "Saving All My Love for You," by Whitney Houston. "I Hate You When I Love You," by Celine Dion. "You Mean the World to Me," by Toni Braxton. "Obsession," by Sarah Vaughan. The combination of the singer's powerful voice and the song's haunting lyrics can arrest you in your tracks. Before you know it, you're singing along and swaying to the sound by the sheer force of the emotion in the singer's voice— you are awash in her emotional agony over the way her man leaves her in knots, or you find yourself recalling the suffering of your own tied-up soul. The song stops playing on the jukebox, but its inference finds root in a foolish girl's heart: It isn't love unless the one you love is incapable of appreciating all the love you've poured into the relationship and unless you're utterly helpless to break free of his mysterious hold on you.

Amazing, isn't it? The same songs on the lips of a man would not have the same impact on an audience. A man drooling over a woman in the same way the Shulammite drools over the elusive shepherd would be embarrassing. While society expects men to be transparent about their sexual desires, it doesn't know what to do with men who talk openly about their feelings as the Shulammite does. Love is women's work (conversely, sex is considered men's work). You and I are expected to notice when love is waning and to care about fixing it, and to anguish over what to do about stirring the embers around until the flames start up again. It's the Shulammite who frets about the romance.

Imagine this: No matter how much the women in my book club enjoy thrashing around a good book that sheds fresh insight on the civil rights movement, the future of the planet, or the plight of education in urban cities, no one finds an excuse to leave the discussion when the book of the month deals with some aspect of romance or relationships between the sexes. Have you ever noticed how much time women, otherwise smart women even, spend talking and thinking about relationships and worrying about what we did or didn't do to deserve the relationships we're in?

Some years ago the novelist Alice Walker assembled a collection of short stories under the title *In Love and Trouble*. Reading story after story of abandonment, lunacy, heartbreak, and relationship violence, Walker's point was obvious: Women in love with men and all things male are women who are in trouble. What an absurd notion to ponder when you're a twentysomething Christian woman as I was back when I first got my hands on the book. Of course, that wasn't my experience of love at the time. Every man I fell in love with back then was charmed by my headstrong ways. But then I turned thirty-five, and fewer and fewer men thought my stubborn ways were cute. The time had come for me to shut up. I am ashamed to say that I tried. But then I turned forty, and I gave up trying to stuff my true self down my own throat. You play the maiden for as long as you can, and then the moment comes when you look in the mirror and realize that you're no longer a maiden. No more pretending that you're dumber than you are. Instead of hanging a shingle on your forehead that says, "I want to get married," as you were inclined to do when you were younger and frequenting bars and hiring dating services to keep you in the mix, time has made you more discriminating about your choices and changed the way you see yourself. "I want to meet someone who is ready to explore a relationship with a woman who is fun, feisty, funny, ambitious, passionate, high-achieving, who enjoys sleeping late on the weekend, and needs a cookbook to fry an egg," is how the personal ad might now read.

Readers have been drawn to the Shulammite down through the centuries because she is a passionate woman who sets her mind on what she wants and goes after it (even though she comes to have a better appreciation of her true worth by the book's end and changes what she expects of her lover in the process). Her passion is unmistakable. Her determination is admirable. The tenacity and energy with which she approaches life make us take notice of her. We are drawn to passionate people like the Shulammite. They arouse our interest with the incredible life energy they exhibit in everything they do. They remind us how much more absorbing and fulfilling life can be. For every woman who has found herself staring blankly into space and unable to come up with anything satisfying to say when asked, "What do you want out of life?" or "What do you want God to help you with most?," the black-skinned maiden in Song of Solomon serves as our role model for trusting your dreams and not being afraid to invent yourself as you go along.

Later editors did her a disservice by lumping her with Solomon's harem. The woman in Song of Solomon gives no indication that she's been duped or hoodwinked into romance. She is her own woman. The feisty damsel in Song of Solomon captures our imagination because we recognize ourselves in this woman's search for something she feels will make her vibrant, fully alive. The experience of falling in love, feeling passion coursing through your body, even the act of sex itself, inspires one to believe that there's more to life. For certain, being willing to elevate another person's happiness and welfare over your own is part of what it means to love someone. It means as well knowing where you end and the other person begins, and vice versa, in this relationship. But bearing up under the winepress of intimacy also means learning to let the give-and-take of love become a springboard for personal development.

These are the love songs that only recently women have found the courage and voice to sing out loud: *I love you, but I can and will survive without you.* It takes a lifetime of unlearning and stripping away at the labels that have been assigned to us to get at the truth. But it can be done. If you're a woman, you can wake up one day and decide that while you're still committed to love, you don't want to have to live without large chunks of yourself in order to be loved and taken seriously. You want yourself back. You don't want your greatest creativity to be swallowed up by someone else's vision. You want to be heard, and you want your lyrics to stand on their own. You want love, but not if it means that you have to pretend to be someone you'd rather not be.

Reflections on The Self

Early in this chapter you find the words: *The moment comes when you have to decide for yourself who you are and what your own desires and fantasies are.*

1. Take the time right now to describe in your own words who you are. How would you describe yourself?

_____

_____

_____

_____

_____

2. Don't be afraid. Don't be ashamed. Open your heart to life's possibilities by boldly declaring what your dreams and hopes are for your life.

_____

_____

_____

_____

_____

3. How much of yourself have you given away over the years for the sake of love? What will it cost you, do you think, to reclaim those lost parts of yourself?

_____

_____

_____

_____

_____

Identity

"God, is that you? I didn't know."

Your desire for a full and fulfilling life will see to it that not only must you speak up and talk about your own desires, but you will also have to find a way to set the record straight and describe in your own words, however eloquently or ineloquently, the journey of mind, body, and soul that has nudged you into the woman you are today. It's that moment in life when as a woman you must peel back all the layers of false selves that have accumulated over the years and finally put into words who you really are. You must describe in your own words who you are and are not, tell what you believe and what you no longer believe. It's the moment when the Shulammite within rises from the ashes.

You catch yourself one day staring at the gently worn, wizened face staring back at you in the mirror, but when you ask yourself, "Who's the fairest of all?," there will be no hesitation as to the answer. "I am," you declare. And it will be true. After years of choosing unwisely, you will finally get it right. The Shulammite knows at last who she is. No more trying on other people's labels. Despite all the temptations to cave in and to be what others want you to be, after trying to live up to other people's definitions of beauty, you are finally desperate to be yourself. And even if you still aren't quite sure at the moment exactly who you are in that inner core, you're content to stay open to life and to God's direction for those experiences that bring the knowing that's needed. As the novelist Zora Neale Hurston once wrote, "There are years that ask questions, and there are years that answer."

It may seem like a small thing to us as modern readers but our heroine is the only woman in Scripture who describes herself in her own words: "I am black and beautiful" (1:5). What a mouthful! Unlike the matriarchs Leah and Rachel, the Shulammite does not come to us through the eyes of a male narrator (Genesis 29). Unlike Tamar, she is not forced to disguise who she really is to avoid rejection (Genesis 38). Unlike Ruth, she does not apologize for being noticed, conspicuous, or different (Ruth 2:10). The Shulammite is unapologetic about who she is. She is "black and beautiful."

You've probably noticed by now that there's some disagreement as to how to translate the Shulammite's description of herself. The Hebrew is equivocal. The Hebrew conjunction *waw* can be translated "but" and "and." The translator is free to translate based on context and her or his own predilections. Not surprisingly, how *waw* is translated here in 1:5 has made an enormous amount of difference in the Western part of the hemisphere. To those translating Song of Solomon from Hebrew into Elizabethan English on behalf of King James I in the seventeenth century (a translation that would come to be known as the King James Version), there was no way of conceiving anyone of dark complexion describing herself as beautiful except in defensive, apologetic tones: "I am black, but comely [beautiful]." (Note that between the sixteenth and twentieth centuries, Britain acquired the largest overseas empire the world has ever known, which included colonizing parts of Africa.) Three hundred and fifty years later some modern translators continue to translate 1:5 in similar fashion, "Dark I am, yet lovely." Other translators, aware that the Hebrew conjunction is in fact neutral in the matter, have shown more enlightenment when they have translated the verse, "I am black *and* beautiful." They are correct. Nothing in the Shulammite's attitude throughout the book suggests that she perceived her complexion as a deterrent or obstacle to her being desirable. Bouyed by the flattery her lover heaps on her, the black-skinned maiden is convinced of her beauty and desirability.

She is by her own admission a woman of dark complexion, but that's nothing strange given the part of the world in which she lived. The hot Mediterranean sun has seen to it that those born beneath her rays are typically olive to dark brown in complexion. But evidently the Shulammite is darker than usual. She explains that her brothers forced her, in retaliation for some offense she doesn't go into, to work outdoors in the sun (1:6), which evidently made her already dark skin only darker. The Shulammite doesn't apologize for her dark complexion, so much as she uses the occasion to protest her brothers' power over her. If she sounds defensive, it's because she's disappointed in her brothers. She resents their power over her. Nothing in the rest of her poetry suggests she feels any shame about the color of her skin.

> *Do not stare at me because I am dark, because the sun*
> *has gazed on me.*
> *My mother's sons were angry with me;*
> *they made me keeper of the vineyards;*
> *but my own vineyard I have not kept!*
>
> (1:6)

Like lots of other women in the Bible, we never have the pleasure of discovering the Shulammite's true name. The daughters of Jerusalem whom she mentions here in 1:5 refer to our heroine by the label *Shulammite* (6:13), but that's all we have in terms of a name that isn't a name in the end, but a reference to her place of birth. What else do we know about the Shulammite? What kind of woman is this in the Bible who talks openly about her desires? Where does she get the courage to speak so frankly about her fantasies? We can never know for sure. Speaking one's mind comes easier for some than others. But with practice, speaking up can be learned. I see this every day in my classroom as a professor.

The young women in my graduate classes are frequently slow to speak up and voice their opinions when there are young men in the class who hold strong and definite views. Not having read the homework assignment is no deterrent to my male students when the time comes to bounce around ideas and propose solutions. But women students are different. They tend to speak up only when they feel confident that the answer they have is the one you're looking for. But what about the many times in class and in life when there are no easy, straightforward textbook-generated answers? Sometimes all that exists is the soft, watery, unformed substance of a hunch, an opinion, and an idea to go on. Whatever truth there is out there waiting to be found will come once you step out and risk everything on that hunch. But how do I get young female students to do the work of talking up, finding their voice, and risking themselves before a bunch of pompous, pugnacious males who stand ready to pounce on every idea? It becomes my task as a teacher to create the environment in which every student feels it is safe and comfortable to test out and banter around unformed ideas. I may turn to one of the female students in the class and ask her point blank if she has any thoughts on the topic; and no matter how tentative her speech, no matter how ineloquent she sounds at first, I am careful to nod, smile, and say some-thing positive as she takes the plunge to speak her mind. Coach her enough times, and eventually neither you nor she remembers a time when she wasn't one to risk an opinion.

> *Let him kiss me with the kisses of his mouth!*
> *For your love is better than wine, your anointing oils*
> *   are fragrant,*
> *your name is perfume poured about.*
> *Which explains why maidens love you.*
>
> (1:2–3)

Stumbling upon her fantasies centuries after she first spoke or recorded them, we find ourselves arrested by the Shulammite's boldness. Her admissions of longing are without apology and without parallel elsewhere in the Bible. It's actually difficult to stop reading Song of Solomon once you stumble upon the unnamed woman's juicy poems. After all, who can resist gazing upon someone caught red-handed in the throes of passion? She brings to mind the hot and sexually forward woman known only as Potiphar's wife, who tried in vain to seduce Joseph the patriarch (Genesis 39). She reappears here in the form of the Shulammite minus the disgrace that marks her story in Genesis.

The woman in Song of Solomon serves also as some-thing of a forerunner to the Samaritan woman in John 4 who is cast as someone who had more husbands than considered decent for a respectable woman. We meet the Samaritan woman forced to draw water at the community well in the middle of the day so as presumably to avoid the stares and whispers of the respectable townswomen. The Shulammite steps onto the pages of biblical history to create a space for women like the wife of Potiphar and the Samaritan woman. She comes on the scene as headstrong and full of passion, and challenges our notions of female decency, respectability, and honor. She pushes us to ask ourselves why a woman's character must always be tied to her chastity. A woman who talks freely about her sexual history is shameless, but a man who does the same is passionate and uninhibited. Perhaps the time has come to rethink our ideas about women and sex. Why can't a woman be both passionate and pious? Why must every popular image of devout women portray them as passive, passionless, and modest? What are we to think of the Shulammite in Song of Solomon? To think that her fantasies and desires have been preserved here in Scripture *without comment, without censure, and without criticism* makes us want to know more about her. They also make us wonder about where we got our notions of womanhood from.

I believe the Shulammite poems have been preserved to cure us of the charge that women love too much. The inference of her book is that it's precisely our ability to love deeply as women that makes us special, unique, holy, and akin to our Creator. We love so much just as

God so loves the world. We are reminded not to be ashamed of our desire to love and for love, but at the same time we are challenged that in our quest for love not to cease loving ourselves. After all, love will fool you. It's apt not to behave the way you expect.

Every time I read the Shulammite's poems, I am reminded of every woman in my neighborhood when I was a girl who was branded as outrageous and spoken about in hushed tones by the so-called decent women in the community. Indecent. Loose. Ungodly. Brazen. Shameless. Hussy. What did a woman have to do in my neighborhood to earn herself such epithets? Nothing much from what I could tell as a child, except not care what men and other women thought of her. That Mrs. Jeannette wore short, tight pants and see-through blouses when she stepped out to put her trash in the garbage can; that Miss Ida Mae played her stereo music loud, smoked openly, and slept with other women's husbands (supposedly); and that Miss Dot sold gin from her back porch and when angered could outcurse any man— made them all the type decent women sucked their teeth at when they walked by or when their names came up in conversation.

I couldn't get enough of these female pariahs when I was growing up. I studied these the way some children apply themselves to learn the rules of decimals and fractions. I was fascinated with the way they applied their lipstick, the way they pinned their hair into a French roll, the way they dabbed perfume across their breasts, the way they walked down the street with their backs straight and their heads in the air, fully aware of the gossip spoken about them from behind closed curtains. Above all, by watching the way they bonded, came to each other's rescue, and protected one another from male intrusions, I learned my earliest lesson in women's friendships. As far as I was concerned, Mrs. Jeannette, Miss Ida Mae, and Miss Dot were some of the most intelligent, courageous, honest, trustworthy women in the neighborhood. I should know. After all, they were my mom's best friends, and as such they were in and out of our apartment almost every weekend laughing, playing cards, cleaning collard greens, thinking up numbers to play, braiding my and my sister's hair, and asking to use the telephone of whoever had managed to pay their bill that week. Certain excesses in my own mother saw to it that she always fell out of favor with the decent women. Eventually she surrounded herself with whatever class of indecent women that existed in the neighborhoods we moved into. I guess you can say then that my mother was to some what you might call indecent and outrageous. She was my first example.

While her well-publicized excesses would usually cost me a friend or two (once friends' mothers figured out who my mother was, I was usually uninvited to whatever I'd been invited to at their house), I am grateful to my mother for the band of shameless, brazen women she surrounded herself with, whom I grew up thinking of as my godmother, play mother, and surrogate mother. These women taught me that it really is possible to survive being shunned, gossiped about, and labeled a shameless hussy by the upstanding women around you. After all, in my neighborhood shameless women were usually the ones upstanding women turned to to protect them from their abusive husbands. Decent women ran to Miss Ida Mae's house at night to get away from their violent husbands, who wouldn't dare try busting down the door of Miss Ida Mae. Everyone knew she kept a pistol under her pillow. How many times did I witness my mother taking in the children of the upstanding woman next door when her husband in a drunken fit was brandishing a gun and threatening to blow her brains out if she didn't jump to whatever request he'd made earlier in the evening. These women didn't dare speak to women like Miss Ida Mae and my mother during the day, but at night when drunk, abusive husbands would come home from work or from gambling away all the money, decent and indecent women alike would put away the differences between them. Women like Miss Ida Mae and my mother stepped in to do what they could not because they were any less fearful of abusive men, but because they figured out there was strength in numbers and there isn't much sense in putting too much stock in labels and what folks think of you. After all, labels traffic in partial truths. No epithet can do justice to the journey that leads a woman to make the choices that she does.

The Shulammite holds out hope that a certain beloved shepherd who remains unknown will be different.

Tell me, you whom my soul loves,
where do you pasture your flock,
where you make it rest at noon.

(1:7)

She refuses to play the role of the respectable young lady. She wants out from under the domination of her household. She will learn that lovers cannot rescue you from you. But at least she has what it takes to survive. She isn't afraid to ask for what she wants.

Sustain me with raisins,
refresh me with apples;
for I am sick with love.
If only his left hand were under my head,
and his right hand embraced me.

(2:5–6)

Thank God for the feisty, passionate woman who penned these provocative poems. She did all of us a service by refusing to keep quiet about her desire for love. Her boldness forces every woman who comes in contact with her poems to examine her own history with love. She forces us to ask ourselves what falling in love, what the experience of feeling loved unconditionally by someone, and finally being wounded by and reunited with the one we love taught us. There were sure to be those who took great exception to the prospect of including in the Bible what amounts to a journal filled with a woman's deepest longings. But evidently there were those who saw some important similarities between erotic desire and a healthy spirituality. The quest for love is a heroic journey full of revelations about God, self, the other, and life itself. The similarities between sexuality and spirituality are not to be ignored, the Shulammite insists. Both depend upon desire to fuel them, as well as all the promises, dreams, restlessness, longing, and spells of absence that heighten desire.

The erratic nature of the poetry in Song of Solomon—the fact that the poems jump from speaker to speaker without transitions, making it frequently difficult for a reader to determine who is speaking (the woman, her beloved, or the girlfriends who seem to be looking on)—only heightens the book's drama. It is impossible to keep up with the lovers. But isn't that just like love, certainly lusty new love? Time blurs. Personalities mesh. Speech trails off. Emotions are hijacked. The scenery goes out of focus. Friends like the "daughters of Jerusalem" who witness the affair and try interjecting some common sense and wisdom at key points ultimately fade into the background (5:9, 6:1, 13). All that matters is the lovers and love itself.

The same goes for the spiritual journey. That first acquaintance with a reality larger than anything you've known before. That first encounter with the Holy. That first moment of recognition that your life has not been senseless, that in fact it has been proceeding along a course that has more intelligence, more meaning, more direction than you ever perceived before. You see all the ways things could have turned out, but they didn't. You are stronger than you imagined. You've been standing on holy ground all this time and didn't know it. You can barely take it all in. A flood of tears wells up. "God, is that you? I didn't know." You ask for forgiveness for all the years you didn't know. You want to bask in the presence of this new knowing for hours. But that's not possible. The time comes to put down your pen and close your journal. End your devotions. Gather your things and return to the mundane world. You wish you could stay. But you can't. Relationships, obligations, and deadlines await you. But you return as a different person. You know better. You have the memory of sweeter glorious moments alone with God and with your self to draw on and to nourish you.

Something in her poetry convinces me that the Shulammite was young when she was in the throes of composing her poems to the shepherd. She seems convinced that love will rescue her from a miserable past. But it doesn't. Your past isn't something for you to be rescued from. Your past is what you learn from as you figure out how to integrate those lessons into the you you're still becoming.

Sometimes I wish I could go back to the young woman I was in my twenties. Mind you, I don't miss my twenties. I don't long to return to my twenties. I can live without all that drama. I'm quite content to be in my forties today. I like who I am now. I didn't like me in my twenties. But if I'd known then what I know now, I wouldn't have been so hard on myself. I could have spared myself all the recriminations I heaped on myself. Sometimes it's good to sit down and write a letter to your younger self. Tell your younger self what you wish you'd known then but didn't. If I could at fortysomething write a letter to myself at twentysomething, here's what I would tell myself:

Dear Renita,

Lighten up and don't be so hard on yourself. Things come together. You learn. You will figure it out. You don't have to be so impatient, so intolerant, so unforgiving of others. One strike is all you permit those who hurt and disappoint you. You don't want to be hurt, so you're quick to dismiss folks. You don't want to be left, so you leave first. People are frail, and so are you. You will survive being hurt. Surviving, moving on, and learning what you need will become important themes in your message years from now.

I see you standing on a crowded #3 subway clutching the strap, trying to hold on as the train jerks and lurches, trying not to fall over into the lap of the man sitting just beneath you. You are trying with everything in you to stand there with poise, not jerk and lurch with the train, but it's hard. So hard. Appearing sturdy is important. You're afraid someone will figure out that you're really scared and unstable. You're trying to stay on your feet, but you have so few models for doing so. You're watching others to see how it's done. How do I tell you that years from now others will be watching you to see how it's done? And you'll have to tell them about all the lurches and jerks that threw you across the train and bore you to where you are today.

You don't believe this right now. You are your mother's daughter, but you are not your mother. Your secrets will not die with you. You will not die thinking you are unlovable. You will not die thinking what you've done can't be forgiven. You will not die unconvinced of your own strength and beauty. You will not be unable to talk about your life. You will find your voice and will spend your wise woman years helping other women—in memory of Ms. Carrie, your mother—find their own God-given voice.

The Shulammite's search for true love is in the end a search for herself. Although her beloved's elusiveness leaves her exasperated and frustrated, she finds herself in the end a different woman than she was when she first embarked on this journey. In the end, the book leaves the passion between the two sweethearts unconsummated. She beckons to him one last time to join her (8:13–14). Whether he does, there is no mention. Those who saw in the book parallels with the spiritual journey probably interpreted the book's end as confirmation of what they saw in the spiritual quest: There's no such thing as consummation, not really. There's only more seeking and growing. Our heroine is still discovering new things about herself at the end of the book. That's because nothing matures a maiden into a woman like impeded love. Nothing sparks the spiritual quest like suffering and dissatisfaction. Indeed, all husbands and lovers are a form of death to the women who love them in that they force the women out of maidenhood and into a maturity they never saw coming, just as suffering is a form of death to the seeker. Love is likely to tear you to bits but it has its creative possibilities. By the book's end, after a "lifetime of loving," the Shulammite—like most women—grows up, becoming wiser, stronger, and more aware of her own gifts than she probably ever thought possible at the beginning of the book. She is a marked woman. She is forever in the process of becoming and never quite satisfied with the results because of her determination not to squelch her desires, but indeed follow her passions.

By the end of the book, we find out the price of loving and living passionately. The Shulammite is a different woman when we find her in the last chapter. Love hasn't come out the way she intended. She's no closer to consummating her affair with the shepherd than she was in the first chapter. But she's not as defensive about what's going on in her life as she was. If this relationship doesn't work, she's no longer quick to assume the fault. If her brothers are as spiteful and critical as ever (8:8–9), she no longer feels it necessary to believe what they say about her. The cost of loving and living passionately means disciplining yourself to accept a life that keeps you somewhere on the edge between searching and finding, fantasy and fulfillment, want and satisfaction. The Shulammite learns the value of her vineyard (8:12), that is, her own self-worth and all the goodness and godness within her, when she stops demanding from her elusive sweetheart what he could never give her and accepts the relationship for what it is. At the book's end, she is still enamored of her paramour; after all, she invites him once more to make haste and join her (8:14). But the desperation is no longer there. Her fear of being alone is gone.

When you have grown strong and wise enough, the things that once caused you pain and exasperation become a complementary part of your being and no longer tear you into pieces. The relationships you once couldn't bear to live without, the decisions that once severed your heart, the not knowing you couldn't abide have become integrated into the new you that you've become by faith. You know who you are. You know your worth. You are willing to risk offending others in order to set the record straight about who you are and all it took to get you to where you are today. The prime task of the journey has been accomplished, which is learning to appreciate both the spiritual and the physical framework of your life. Both have gone into producing the great work of art that is your own life. You can finally claim the journey that brought you to who and where you are. At last you can look back and recognize that it was God all along nudging you at critical junctures, whispering, "Take another look in the mirror. There's more to you than even you know."

Reflections on Identity

In this chapter you find the words: *Your past isn't something for you to be rescued from. Your past is what you learn from as you figure out how to integrate those lessons into the you you're still becoming.*

1. If you'd known ten, twenty or thirty years ago what you know now, what would you have done differently?

_____

_____

_____

_____

_____

2. Use the example of the journal entry on pages 44–45 to write a letter to the self you were ten or twenty years ago. What assurances and comfort would you want to offer the woman you were then that might help her to forgive herself, to not be so hard on herself, to instruct her, or to encourage her?

_____

_____

_____

_____

_____

_____

_____

3. What are you absolutely passionate about these days?

_____

_____

_____

_____

_____

Truth

~~~
❦
~~~

"To speak up for the pleasures of love and against the injustices of life itself is to speak up for everything that God loves and represents."

Your desire for a full and fulfilling life will meet with success only as you are able to do the difficult work of unlearning what you have been taught about pleasing others. You have to give up any lingering need you have to be liked and accepted by everyone. A desire for other people's approval has to be replaced by a preparedness to face rejection and scorn as the price for following your compass and following your passions.

Prejudice is what the black-skinned Shulammite in Song of Solomon encounters throughout the book as we watch her struggle continuously to strike a balance between her desire to be loved and her effort to retain some dignity as a woman. Her poems craftily invite us as her audience to confront our deepest held prejudices, four of them in particular. First, in a culture that ranks skin color, the Shulammite makes us look at our prejudices against women with dark, dark complexions. Second, she makes us examine our prejudices against women on the low end of the economic totem pole who have to do day work, menial work, and back-breaking labor to pay their bills. Third, her refusal to keep silent about her treatment makes us come clean about the way we feel about women who tell it like it is. And fourth, we have to confront the stereotypes we've inherited from our society of passionate women who know what they want then throw modesty to the wind and go after it. Especially when "it," or at least part of it, is an intimate relationship with a man, or as the late Nina Simone put it, "a little sugar in my bowl." The book's aim is to convince readers, both male or female, to recognize themselves in the dark-skinned maiden, to identify with her desire to be understood and appreciated for her own worth, and to confront their own prejudices.

Patriarchy isn't the word the Shulammite uses to describe the world in which she has grown up, but it's okay if we describe it that way. You don't have to be a feminist to find the word a useful one for talking about how societies organize themselves in ways that favor maleness over femaleness. Thinking women of faith have been grappling for centuries for ways to talk about the unfair way women and girls are treated in society, and we've been hard-pressed to come up with a term that describes the widespread assumptions we encounter in our society about a woman's place and women's roles. I am reminded in particular of a famous speech that outspoken Nannie Helen Burroughs gave in 1900 at a

National Baptist Convention in Richmond, Virginia, entitled, "How the Women Are Hindered from Helping." That speech by then-twenty-one-year-old Burroughs led to a separate Women's Department being founded that year in the denomination to address the needs of women in the church, with Burroughs as part of its leadership. Burroughs didn't use the word *patriarchy* to describe the injustice she felt Baptist women experienced in their churches, but she didn't bite her tongue when enumerating the sins of the men of the church against its female members. The belief that women are inferior to men is at the heart of patriarchal attitudes toward women. Thinking women know that beliefs become norms, and norms become structures, and structures become "just the way things are." Women with the courage to stand up and speak the truth to the powers that be are the ones who force us to confront our attitudes and who force systems to bend where previously they resisted bending. We sometimes stammer when we have to talk about our passions because we are unaccustomed to thinking about passion in ways other than anything having to do with sex and romance. But passion is more than sex and romance. It's about the life energy, the inner flame, with which you approach life as a whole.

Coming to grips with the fact that there will be lots of people who will not like you for speaking the truth is a hard reality for many women to face. We would rather face death than disapproval. It's an affliction especially peculiar to females raised in patriarchal societies. We don't want to be troublemakers. Women who don't know when to shut up are the greatest threat to the status quo. Those are the women for whom sermons from Proverbs about nagging women are directed rather than ones about the feisty woman of Song of Solomon. "It is better to live in a corner of the housetop than in a house shared with a contentious wife" (Proverbs 25:24) is a Scripture a visiting preacher once preached about in my church when I was growing up that left me scratching my head as to what kind of woman he was talking about. "What's a 'contentious' wife?" I leaned over and asked my stepmother. "A woman who figures out that she's married to a fool," she mumbled under her breath. The women in my small church sat stiff and quiet throughout the sermon, including Sister Nettie, who always shouted and disrupted things after the preacher read his Scripture for the morning. When Sister Nettie refrained from saying anything in the sermon, I knew things were serious. Choruses of "Amen" and "Say it, Preacher" rang out through the sanctuary. The men who normally nodded and slept during the preacher's message and sneaked out for cigarette breaks were alert and boisterous in their support of the morning's message.

Despite all the political, social, and economic gains women have made in the world since the time of the Shulammite, some attitudes have not changed. Men who speak their minds are leaders; women who speak up are troublemakers. I am reminded of the stereotypes facing women every time I stand in a pulpit to preach and every time I stand before a class to lecture. There's something about a confident woman that's bound to rankle some people. If rankling folks bothers you, you'll never get through the second page of your printed speech when you stand to speak. Let's face it: Well-behaved women rarely change history.

A soul-satisfying life is not something God grants some women and denies others. The chance for a soul-satisfying life becomes the possibility we long for when we begin to perceive those crossroads moments in our lives when we find ourselves in situations where we must decide what's really important to us. We wake up one day to find ourselves having to decide whether we will choose our path based on our own dreams for ourselves or based on what others think is the best path for us. The Shulammite's poems become our poetic guide into what I have identified as ten pivotal, deeply personal moments in a woman's life when we find ourselves forced, whether by God or by circumstance, into situations where what we choose and who we will become are inextricably linked.

In the previous chapters a lot has been said about the fact that our heroine is forthright and outspoken. But let's dig deeper and get to the bottom of the matter. It's not just that a woman talking back causes a writer like the one behind the book of Proverbs to target her for ridicule. It's the fact that she won't be intimidated into backing down and keeping quiet that sends her detracters into a froth.

"No, I don't like the way you touch me when other students aren't around."

"Yes, I could loan you the money; but I don't want to."

"No, I don't appreciate the way you spoke to me in front of everyone in the office."

"Yes, I do love you. But I also love myself enough to know when something or someone is not in my best interest."

Whenever you decide to speak up and not be a doormat, and not to be intimidated into recanting, you had better be prepared for your approval ratings to go down exponentially. Big-mouthed women are a turnoff. In the literature my fifth grade daughter reads, mouthy, fearless girls are, according to the boys they compete with, right up there with toad soup. Aggressive women are impossible to get along with. Being fearless is unattractive in women. (Even my husband with all his talk about being attracted to headstrong women, which is mostly true, takes lots of pleasure in the fact that I'm terrified of reptiles of any form and rely upon him to do most of the talking to service people when we travel. He'll deny it, of course, when he reads this.) Women with strong opinions who are approaching forty have a better chance of being taken hostage by terrorists than getting married, according to the stereotype. Strong, outspoken women are only men-hating lesbians, or so I'm reminded from time to time.

"I figured that if you could marry, then there was still a chance that I could marry," a friend confessed to me over lunch months after my wedding. I think she meant it as a compliment. But it didn't sound like one right then. I sat quietly sipping my cranberry juice mulling over her meaning. Are the chances of a thirty-seven-year-old single woman marrying that much of an unlikelihood? Or was there something about me in particular that made it impossible to believe that I would ever marry? Am I that homely? I wondered. A college friend's words over the phone earlier when she'd heard that I was engaged came back to my mind: "Girl, I just gotta meet the man who's gonna marry you!" What made me so unmarriageable in the minds of my friends? Was I such a headstrong, opinionated, and independent woman that my friends couldn't imagine a man ever falling in love with me? They just couldn't imagine how I was going to pull off being married and continue to be a headstrong woman. To tell you the truth, I wasn't sure how I was going to do it myself. After all, I'd grown up hearing the same messages they had.

"Is your husband your head in your marriage?" a radio commentator asked me recently. "No, I had a head of my own already when I got married," I answered. "So, I guess you're one of those women libber types. You wear the pants in your house, huh?" he hurled at me with enough contempt in his voice that, had it happened ten years ago, it would have made me stumble over myself trying to explain what I did and didn't mean by that remark. But I'm not that girl anymore. Ten years later I sat quietly and allowed my refusal to be snared into a debate on a syndicated radio show about my marriage to speak for itself. Despite what people think, I don't say everything that comes to mind. If I had that afternoon, I'm sure the radio station would have lost its license.

It was an old ploy. A surefire way to silence a woman with a mind of her own is to question her sexuality. Any woman who refuses to be silent, who questions male authority as a given, who thinks that women and men were created as equals, by God, must want to be a man herself. Ten to fifteen years ago I would have worked overtime to expunge any such notion about myself from the record: Lesbian. Femi-nazi. Get back in line! Who do you think you are? I am embarrassed to admit that I've done my share of apologizing, explaining, and back-tracking over the years trying to offer a more pleasing portrait of myself to the public. Did I mention that the interviewer that night was a Christian radio announcer? I could hear the charge "Crucify her" and "Stone her" in every question he hurled in my direction. I am a miscreant because I am a thinking woman of faith, while he gets held up as a loyal Christian as he spews venom and insults at me in the name of divine truth. There's a price to be paid for challenging the status quo. I forget, but luckily there's always someone from the Christian right around to remind me. You can't go around breaking molds and expect to be applauded when some folks loved and cherished those molds. There's bound to be a price on your head for stepping out of line. No matter how much you tell yourself that you're accustomed to the jeers and accusations, even at fifty, there's always something that remains to be said that can still sting you, or someone you expected to understand you whose rejection cuts you to the bone. But you heal, and thank God for the new friends and sources of strength you find in the places where society consigns the people it disapproves of.

Imagine how impoverished Scripture would be if we didn't have the example of the Shulammite. From the book's beginning to its end, the feisty black-skinned maiden stands up to the powers that be that do their best to snare her into acquiescence. Her brothers put her out to work in the hot sun, whether as a prank or punishment is unclear. She complains and searches for happiness outside her home. When by the book's end love fails to deliver on all its promises, she is reminded that she doesn't measure up (8:8). Her family frets that their sister's small breasts might interfere with her brideprice when (if) the occasion arises that a suitor comes seeking her in earnest.

> *We have a little sister, and she has no breasts.*
> *What shall we do for our sister,*
> *On the day when suitors come to see her?*

(8:8)

Since laboring in the vineyard in the hot sun at the book's opening didn't succeed in breaking her spirit, perhaps lashing out at her sense of self-esteem at the book's close will. Although our heroine as a maiden remains according to the rules of her culture under her brothers' guardianship, she does not remain the same woman she started off as when the book opened. Love did not turn out as she'd hoped, but still she doesn't let that make her crumble when her brothers tease her. By the book's end, she still holds out hope that she and her sweetheart will find each other; but she doesn't appear by the book's close likely to wilt away if that doesn't happen. Romance comes and goes, but passion has a way of sparking an inner flame in a woman that doesn't die out easily. Love hurts when it's over, but what it awakened when it was alive is not easily quenched. The Shulammite's poems have been passed down to us, I want to believe, as a way of championing not a passion for love, but for life itself. To love is to live, to hope, to cherish, and to believe in new possibilities. To love life is to love God. To speak up for the pleasures of love and against the injustices of life itself is to speak up for everything that God loves and represents.

Our heroine in Song of Solomon forces us to confront head-on our deepest prejudices about women who refuse to be defeated by love (or the lack of love in their lives). In her case, she refuses to defer to others and insists upon speaking up. From the outset of the book, the Shulammite speaks openly about her victimization by her family members. They put her to work in the hot blazing Mediterranean sun. Not to teach her the discipline of work, but in retaliation against something she said or did. What her offense was, she doesn't say. She simply asserts that they were angry with her for something. If the eight chapters of the book are any indication of the poet's personality, then she's not a woman who backs down easily. The Mediterranean men in her family consigned her to work in the vineyard as a way of putting her in her place and teaching her a lesson. But the Shulammite refused to bite her tongue. She complains that she's been forced into work she didn't choose. She is a victim of the power her society permits her family members to have over sisters and men to have over women. She complains and throws her energies into creating a life that will take her away from her family's rule.

In the end, the Shulammite does not allow herself to be defined by the opinions of others. She insists that her body is fine the way it is, thank you (8:10). She refuses to let them tell her who she is. She is who she says she is. "I am invincible (to your definitions, anyway), and I am at peace with my breasts just the way they are," she says in essence. She is the only woman in Scripture who describes herself in her own words (1:1–5; 8:10). Her resolve forces us to face our prejudices and stereotypes. She challenges the dominant aesthetic (1:5). She pooh-poohs the culture's standards of beauty (1:6). She confronts the stereotypes about class and romance (1:6). She is unapologetic about the way she looks and relaxes in her beloved's desire for her. She insists that her beloved's desire is for her only, despite what others think (7:10). This is the talk of a woman who is under pressure both to conform and to relinquish her rights to be loved by the man of her choice. She leaves us scrambling to decide: Do we endorse her quest to find satisfying love, irrespective of where such a search might take her? Or do we, along with her gawking audience, allow our stereotypes about black, aggressive, forward women to censure her, impose limits on her, and force her into vineyards not of her choosing (1:6; 8:12)?

The Shulammite is the woman who knows that no matter how much you say you don't care, you do care, and care deeply, that you're branded by others and left feeling isolated for your choices. "Eventually it comes to you," wrote the playwright Lorraine Hansberry, "that which makes you exceptional, if you are at all, is what also makes you lonely." Forced into the skin of a black woman, we are made to see her as neither Amazon nor demon, the two extremes of our prejudices against headstrong women. She becomes every woman who has had to pray to God for the strength to fight against stereotypes and ignore efforts by others to pressure her into keeping silent about the rape, the discrimination, the abuse she has suffered. She insists that she is deserving of love just the way she is and sets out to find a man who is smart and unconventional enough himself to find her attractive. We open our Bibles and turn to the book that bears her tale when we're feeling pressured by family and society to cave in. She tells it like it is, and in doing so she reminds us that if ridicule is our punishment for speaking, then so be it. The truth will set you free, but first it will hurt your feelings. We are grateful for the Shulammite's headstrong, stubborn ways. We can only hope that the shepherd was able to live up to her fantasy when they finally managed to get together. If he didn't, we hope she was able to redirect her energies elsewhere and accept a truth every woman has to learn and relearn a hundred times in her lifetime: *Psst . . . you are the source of your own passion.*

Reflections on Truth

❧

At the heart of this chapter is the line: *Coming to grips with the fact that there will be lots of people who will not like you for speaking the truth is a hard reality for women to face.*

1. What is your greatest fear about telling the truth?

_____

_____

_____

_____

_____

2. Name some people God has placed in your life who are your greatest cheerleaders and others who are your most ardent critics.

_____

_____

_____

_____

_____

3. What is the difference between an arrogant woman and a self-confident woman?

_____

_____

_____

_____

_____

4. Can you name some ways in which prejudice and stereotypes have kept you from opening yourself up to meet new (and different) people?

_____

_____

_____

_____

_____

Balance

❧

*"So why don't you get some help
before you collapse?"*

Your desire for a full and fulfilling life will cause you to regularly weigh your dream of finding a sustaining relationship and having a family of your own against the cold, hard realities of the enormous amount of psychic and physical energy women expend trying to achieve domestic equilibrium. It's not unusual to hear a young woman in a new relationship express shock when she finds out just how much time and energy love demands. She is also surprised to find that she seems to be the only one in the relationship who feels gobbled up by love. Her partner is usually oblivious to this feeling because men tend not to be consumed with and by relationships in the same way as women. That's probably because marriage is not a sacrificial matter to a man in the same way it is to a woman. In a patriarchal society, where men's status over women is supposedly a given, men tend to gain more than they lose when they marry. A man's reputation is enhanced when he weds. He has joined the ranks of those through marrying and siring children who put down roots and begin the task of building a lasting future for themselves. Conversely, it's not so much a woman's stature, but her image as a respectable woman, that is improved upon through marriage. Marriage makes her respectable, but it doesn't improve her credibility as a person. If she isn't careful, she finds herself completely absorbed into her partner's world and has to be reminded of her own dreams and gifts. We are expected to give up parts of ourselves for the pleasure of being married. Nothing is more shocking to the system than to discover that love has bound you to your marriage in a way that he is not.

Reading the poetry in Song of Solomon, one gets the impression that as gentle, seductive, caring, and emotionally transparent as the shepherd comes across in the courtship, it's the Shulammite in the end who is working overtime at making the relationship come together. That may be just because her voice dominates in the book. It may also be because that's just the way it is. Love is women's work, or so it seems. We are expected to make the sacrifices necessary to make relationships work and to keep the home running smoothly. The Shulammite is hopeful that a relationship between the shepherd and herself is possible because she is by the middle of the book still convinced of the power of love and romance to change her fortunes. She wants out from under her family's rule, and she dreams of love as her escape. That's not unusual. But is she setting herself up for a rude awakening? When you depend upon other people to give your life meaning, shape, or excitement, aren't you making them the source of your passion? What makes her certain that she's not exchanging one house ruled by the whims of the men in her family for another house ruled by the whims of the man she loves?

To her credit, however, our maiden is not so taken with love that she's totally unaware of the problems that can set in and completely dismantle the dreams that lovers have. The line "Catch us the foxes, the little foxes, that ruin the vineyards . . ." (2:15) was probably a popular quote or a lyric from a well-known song. It warned lovers to be on guard against the annoyances and invasions that can sneak up on a relationship and choke the romance out of it. A modern quip that may come close in meaning is: "The easiest thing is falling in love. The hardest thing is staying in love." After teasingly asking for a few stolen moments with him (2: 10, 13, 14), she uses the fox quote here to warn her sweetheart to beware of those who may be watching, listening in, or ready to pounce on their romance and undo it before it gets started. Spoken like new lovers, don't you think? She thinks that naysayers are the greatest threat to their relationship. Little does she know that the greatest threat to the relationship lies within, not without. If their love is anything like love as many of us know it, it isn't strangers, but the needs, weaknesses, and flawed expectations of the lovers themselves that pose the greatest threat to the relationship. Little does she know she is right now setting up a pattern in their courtship that is likely to follow her into their marriage, if she doesn't catch it beforehand. "Don't start nothing you don't want to keep up for the rest of your life," one woman's grandmother warned her when she announced her engagement. "If you start out cooking every night and making sure everything is in its place, when you work just as hard during the day, it will be very hard to keep up when the children come and the stress really mounts." The role of the vigilante in the partnership, the one who maintains the relationship by doing whatever it takes to keep things running smoothly, the one who feels it her duty to keep irritations to a minimum, will wear you down. Not to mention that it's a thankless role to take on.

So who and what are the "foxes" the maiden refers to in 2:15? Foxes are pests to those who plant vineyards. Grapes are delectable treats on the landscape that the tiny, clever, feisty, quick scavengers find hard to pass up. They stealthily make their way into the vineyard when no one's watching and nibble away at the clusters of treasure before any trap can catch them. Foxes are fierce and relentless little creatures who do not give up easily on the treats they've set their sights on. They are a ruin to a vineyard just like power games are a ruin to a relationship. Truly nothing eats away at romance like being locked in a battle over whose turn it is to wash the dishes, blaming each other for who forgets to pick up the children on time, and contending that whoever makes the most money should be able to insist upon things being done a certain way. These are the kinds of pesty, persistent disagreements between partners that to outsiders sound like they have simple, easy solutions if the two would just sit down and talk things out. But to the two people involved, it's a deeper matter. It's a question of all the needs, expectations, and dreams each person brings into a marriage and fully expects the other person to meet. "If you loved me, you would(n't) . . ." the two of you scream back and forth to each other just beneath the surface.

Like many women, the Shulammite is unaware that she is setting herself up for the role of the SuperWoman, SuperWife, and SuperMom. It's a role lots of us fall into as women and relish for a while. Oh, we complain that everything falls to us, that the burden of the home and the relationship is on our shoulders. But we take delight in the Hallmark cards we find on our pillow praising us for our sacrifices; the special days in which everyone pitches in to give us a day off; the accolades heaped on us at public gatherings for our ability to keep things going and for wearing so many hats with grace. In the end, token gestures are just that: token gestures. They applaud your ability to function gracefully amid an inequitable balance of power. Token gestures, however, don't change the balance of power.

Study after study shows that working moms and wives experience more stress and depression than do working fathers and working women who are single and childless. The implication is that work itself causes a mother stress and depression and that quitting work and becoming a stay-at-home mom is the remedy. It's not uncommon these days to open a newspaper or magazine, or to turn on the television to find stories about working mothers, especially those in high-level professional jobs, leaving their six-figure-income careers to return home to take care of their families. The women complain of being tired of juggling the demands of work and home. They are bailing out of their careers, or deliberately turning down assignments that could lead to promotion, because they feel that they can no longer afford to give so much of themselves to work and employers that are unsympathetic to the needs of working moms. Some are deciding to bail out and go home because they don't want to miss out on their children's lives. Of course, most of the women featured in these stories are white, upper-class women married to men with jobs that allow their wives the option of leaving their careers to stay home with the kids. The research isn't out yet on whether, or to what extent, women of color who are moms and career women are following their Anglo sisters back to the hearth. In the meantime we are left believing that inflexible employers and the all-or-nothing nature of work are the causes of the stress and depression that working mothers experience.

All focus is on the stress factors outside the home to explain the burden working mothers bear. Little is said about the stress factors we contend with inside the home. No one raises the question why we who are accustomed to wielding enormous power and influence at work fare so poorly at home when it comes to negotiating who does what. No one bothers to take a look at what happens when the time comes for women to negotiate with partners over the emotional, psychological, and sheer physical work needed to create a mutually satisfying home life. The truth is that oftentimes our intense desire to be loved, to have a family, and to be in a lifetime committed relationship make us more willing to sacrifice time and energy in order to make our domestic dreams come true. Wanting equality in the workplace made many of us learn how to speak up for ourselves on the job, and figure out all that it takes to broker power on the job. But how to take some of those same skills home and apply them in our marriages and family is another thing.

The responsibility of caring for children, managing the household, and creating a well-run home life usually falls to the one who cares most about such things. We have worn ourselves ragged at work only to come home to find more work waiting for us on a second shift. If the alternative is an ongoing state of conflict and discord over who does what, we tend to be the one more likely to give in and compromise in order to maintain peace in the home. I am generalizing here, to be sure. This isn't the situation for all women. Some working women actually have supportive partners and families, and have found the support they need from home to make it possible to keep home and career *reasonably* afloat. But conversations I've had over the years with women have convinced me that many, many of us are depleted by the demands of both work and love.

"So why don't you get some help before you collapse?" I asked a thirtysomething mom who was trying to figure out how to launch a new magazine while caring for two young sons and finding time for her lawyer husband, who spent long hours at his desk as a special counsel. "I know I should, but I feel guilty." About what? "About asking for help to do things I know I could do if I had the time and energy to do them." Asking her husband to help out more around the house was a no-no. "I feel guilty about asking him to do anything around the house when he works like a dog already at the office." Making us feel guilty as wives and mothers is one of the most effective weapons in the campaign to keep us in our place. Women entangled in feeling guilty about working, about not working, about needing help with the kids and the house, about noticing that the marriage is falling apart and needing some attending to, make good wives. You're likely to keep quiet about your pain. Apparently, while many of us were off preparing ourselves for opportunities to work in the traditionally male world of high-achieving work, no one was teaching our men how to take on traditionally female domestic tasks at home and to view their taking an active part in the home not as a favor to their wives, but as important and necessary work to building an equitable and loving homelife. No one was helping them learn how to behave differently. Neither was anyone bothering to help either of us learn new ways of *being* in our relationships other than the old way of one person being dominant and the other one submissive.

Here's one that's bound to cause my conservative friends to gnaw on their aprons: Teaching women to submit to their husbands—and using biblical texts out of context to buttress one's argument—has not gotten us very far. It didn't take the Women's Movement of the 1970s to make women question this one. Even before then women were pressing ministers, counselors, and Bible teachers to define exactly what Paul meant by "submission" in Ephesians 5. The very fact that Paul felt it necessary to write his treatise on submission suggests that there were women who thought differently. Women at Corinth and elsewhere had radically different ideas about the balance of power in marriage. They didn't need a feminist movement to tell them that there was something unfair about the expectations placed on them in marriages. Submitting to husbands just because they were male didn't fit with their understanding of what it meant to be new creatures in Christ (2 Corinthians 5:17). Let me just pause here to say that I find it enormously encouraging to know that for as long as women have been told to submit and obey, there have been women who have refused to take such teachings at face value and have questioned, probed, and in many instances outright refused to do what they were told to do. Even before Paul was admonishing the Corinthian women to zip up their ambitions, ancient Hebrew women raised questions and challenged the authorities about the way things were. The five daughters of Zelophedad whose father had died and left them without a male guardian complained about the unfairness of the inheritance laws which excluded daughters from inheriting the property left by their deceased fathers (Numbers 27:8–11). What's the point here? There have always been women who have believed that loving men shouldn't have to mean losing self and forfeiting everything dear.

Of course, those who cling to Paul's writing to uphold their image of marriage as hierarchal quickly point to Paul's injunction in Ephesians 5:25 for husbands to love their wives as something that's supposed to make Paul's injunction to women to submit more romantic and palatable. The inference being, of course, that any woman would gladly submit to a man who loves her as Christ loved the church. Hmmm . . . sounds good on paper perhaps, but what does all this mean? What does it mean to demand that I submit to my husband? What does submission look like in the everyday give-and-take of intimacy where two people must work through the myriad of chores that come with keeping romance alive and keeping a family going? What sense does it make to think that men aren't themselves confused by the injunction to rule over and love women?

Let me make clear that I appreciate Paul's efforts, however blundered, to stabilize relationships between men and women in the New Testament church, and to set the record once and for all on what a Christian household should look like. I can imagine the bedlam that erupted when talk about everyone being a "new creation" spread from house church to house church. Undoubtedly, women who had joined the new liberating movement that a certain late Galilean carpenter had initiated began to feel a kind of freedom of spirit, mind, and heart they'd never encountered before. If it were true that "if anyone be in Christ they are new creatures" (2 Corinthians 5:17), then this new life in the spirit called for everything to be susceptible to reimagining, including relations between the two sexes. Out with the old Hebraic, Greek, and Roman models of men dominating women. "Let's imagine new ways of being in loving healthy relationships in Christ," they probably reasoned. So the feisty women of Corinth refused sex with their husbands on demand (I Corinthians 7), ripped off the veils they wore on their heads (I Corinthians 11), and saw no reason why they should remain silent in church anymore (I Corinthians 14). You go girls!

Women were not the only ones hoping for a new way to relate to the opposite sex. You can bet there were also men (no matter how small the numbers) who were tired of the old straitjacket model of domination and acting macho, men who were willing to experiment with new ways of expressing themselves and being in relationships with women. I look at my father, who turns seventy-two years old this year, and wonder how different old age might have been for him if he had had to learn to take care of himself and hadn't left it to my mother when they were married, my stepmother the brief time they were married, and a host of "women friends" afterward to cook, clean, iron, fold, and put away things for him. For two years he fought against his adult children's pleas that he move to an assisted-living facility where he could get the care he needed, insisting that he could take care of himself. Even though the grime in his apartment made it obvious that he couldn't. At seventy-two it was impossible to teach him to clean up after himself. And now that he's an old man set in his ways, incapable of living alone and ill suited to be living with anyone other than himself, he prefers his own grime and filth to company. Routine personal care deeds that he'd been spared for years and that he never bothered to learn because he was a man forced him into a nursing home in old age.

They were probably a minority of men in biblical times who were willing to reinvent manhood and experiment with new definitions of masculinity that we know little about. Perhaps in the evangelistic team Priscilla and Aquila, we have such a model couple, two people who were both partners in ministry and soul mates (Romans 16:3–5; I Corinthians 16:9; Acts 18:8–9). One partner is never mentioned in Scripture without the other, with Priscilla as the one who's always mentioned first. Even Paul, who elsewhere demanded women to keep silent in church, acknowledges Priscilla and Aquila as "fellow laborers" (Romans 16:3). Evidently Priscilla was a gifted woman in her own right, but that fact didn't seem to bother her husband, Aquila. He seemed willing to share the spotlight with his wife and to enjoy the benefits of mutually working together to build a life and ministry together.

Let's leave the first century and leap forward to the twenty-first century and give credit to the many men who really are struggling to adjust to roles they were not trained for and may not have desired. We are all in transition. But let's face it: That transition is made even more difficult by the fact that this is one of those instances where some of the theology and teachings we've heard in our churches have lagged behind the vision some of us have of building a world for ourselves and for our children where relationships are not characterized by power, domination, and violence. Every time I take out my pen to write or stand to lecture, I am working to create the beloved community that both John the Evangelist and Martin L. King Jr., wrote about. I'm forever trying to leave my daughter a picture of life, love, and community where, contrary to what others say, no one has to be in charge. No one has to be on top and someone else on the bottom.

When did love get equated with power? How did the foxes manage to sneak into our vineyard and start nibbling away at our dreams of living as one? How did women come to equate being loved with being dominated? How did men come to equate love with controlling and threatening those they love? How can you be expected to love someone whom you live in fear of leaving you, of not loving you, of not taking care of you, and of threatening to hurt you if you fail to do what he demands? Who wants to be loved by someone you can't count on to tell you the truth because she is afraid that you'll withdraw from her. What kind of love is this? But this is precisely the kind of love we've constructed for ourselves. No wonder love, a tender fruit in the vineyard, fails at the rate that it does.

Until things change at the macro level, the power battles women and men find themselves locked into at the micro level in their private relations can be negotiated by only one individual woman relating to one individual man. You can't allow the weight of what historically has been all the problems between the sexes to come down on your relationship. This reminds me of the response of a friend who was well into her forties when she first married. I'd asked her, "So, how do you like being married?" "I don't know about what it's like being married," she responded. "All I know is what it's like to be married to the man I married." Life is about choices, to be sure, and no one can expect to "have it all." But the time has come to level the playing field so women can have the same chance at combining family life with meaningful work.

For some of us, having it all doesn't have anything to do with being SuperWoman. It means simply being able to expect to find relationships that do not stunt or diminish you as a woman, but support your best efforts, first, at creating a balanced life for yourself, and second, of bringing the kingdom of God that much closer to reality. It's not that you want it all; you just don't want to be the only one responsible for everyone else having it all. For lots of women, the search for someone to build a life with is a search for *one* someone who is willing to experiment with loving and living with you in ways he's never imagined, but ways he's eager to experiment with. Perhaps that's what the Shulammite meant in the final verses of the same chapter when she closes her ears and eyes to everything and everyone around and insists, "My *beloved is mine, and I am his;* . . ." (2:16). She refuses to be baited into making her sweetheart bear the weight of all the sins and wrongs of "men" and "mankind." Hopefully she also refuses to allow herself to be made to bear the weight of the blindsights of every woman that ever lived.

Finally, the easiest thing is to back off from pursuing a vision of equality in our relationships, given all the painfully complex issues that come up. The stakes are high. And yet, here is where a vision of equality is needed most. It's precisely here in our relationships where the primary and most lasting glimpse of love, joy, faith, community, and the "kingdom of heaven" are worked out. Paul was right about one thing: Love *is* work in as much as "Love is patient. Love is kind; love is not envious or boastful or arrogant or rude. It does not insist on its own way; it is not irritable or resentful . . ." (I Corinthians 13). There's nothing hierarchal or dominating about this kind of love. Why should it be reserved only for the love between friends and neighbors? It sounds like a great place to me for women and men to start in reimagining and rebuilding a basis for romantic love.

Reflections on Balance

We've all fallen prey to the temptation to do it all. *Like many women, the Shulammite is unaware that she is setting herself up for the role of the SuperWoman, Super-Wife, and SuperMom*—take your pick.

1. Sit down and make a list of all the roles you play and hats you wear in a week, a month.

_____

_____

_____

_____

2. Which roles have you fallen into because it was easier than starting a fight? Which ones did you volunteer and take on (not knowing fully all that was involved)?

_____

_____

_____

_____

3. Who are or what is draining your energy these days?

_____

_____

_____

_____

_____

4. What things, as a result of reading this chapter on balance, can you begin to shift, to eliminate, and to start renegotiating in order to achieve more balance in your personal life and more equity in your relationships?

_____

_____

_____

_____

_____

Choices

"On the basis of who you are and what you know, you must make a decision about what path to take."

Your desire for a full and fulfilling life will remain at the level of desire and will never become a reality until you begin to live your life as a choicemaker. Waiting your whole life to be chosen, rescued, loved, noticed, offered a chance, picked for the part, and singled out for love is a sure way to sit by and watch life pass you by. It's also a sure way to spend a great deal of your life feeling like a victim instead of a heroine. The Shulammite could have resigned herself to waiting for love to find her, to remaining a victim of her brothers' bullying, to living in fear. God knows she endures enough in the eight chapters she left us to justify her staying put and giving up on taking chances. But she did not, and neither should we. The Shulammite risked ridicule, criticism, challenge, failure, and embarrassment for the possibility of living a bigger life than the one society assigned to her as a woman. Romance was her chance for escape from her brothers' rule because that was the era in which she lived.

Centuries later, women with far more options available to them than the Shulammite ever had still expect romance to save them from a dull life. But it rarely does. It didn't back then. The black-skinned maiden took a risk and followed her passions. What you risk reveals what you value. That's the real point of her story. Romance doesn't save you; being unafraid to choose, to take risks, to make a decision is what makes it possible for things to turn around in your life. Who knows? Had the chance to travel as a diplomat to exotic regions like the Queen of Sheba, or to study law as a student of Scripture like the prophet Hulda, or to become a disciple like Mary Magdalene to a charismatic teacher been options for the Shulammite, she may have chosen any of these over love. But those weren't her options. Our heroine chose building a life for herself over slaving away in someone else's vineyard. Even if romance failed, there was always the chance that something else would come along. And when and if it did, fortunately she was in the habit of weighing her options and stepping out.

Women who have something of the Shulammite in them are choicemakers. They know how to dive deep within and tap into the inner resources God has given them to help them plot out some strategies for changing their circumstances. Following one's passions doesn't mean haphazardly chasing after every whim that strikes you nor accepting every offer extended you. Being passionate means living your life fearlessly. What if I make a mistake? What if something goes horribly wrong? What if I lose more than I gain? What if I make a fool of myself? After all, choices have consequences. The Shulammite endured ridicule, she was assaulted by the powers that be, she met indecisiveness from the shepherd once she let him in her heart, and she met skepticism from her close friends, the daughters of Jerusalem. Who wouldn't think twice about their decision-making power after putting up with these things? But you either grow or allow yourself to be diminished by the choices you make or choose not to make. The difference between the woman who shirks back at decision-making time and the one who gathers herself up and tries again is that the latter is able to separate what happens to her from what happens within her. Even if she blows it, she never sees herself as a failure at heart. She figures out what she's supposed to learn from her mistakes, and resolves next time to "fail better." Messing up is the risk you take for stepping out. But it's also the feedback we need for how to take pain and use it for growth.

"But doesn't living your life as a choicemaker run counter to some pretty fundamental tenets of our Protestant tradition?" you may be asking. We've been taught that discovering one's vocation and purpose in life means to be called, chosen, and set apart for a particular assignment, often against one's will. Making choices, taking action, and rebounding from failure doesn't allow much room for standing by and seeing yourself as the victim who's waiting for something or someone to rescue you from your condition. "I'm waiting for God to give me a sign before I do anything" is no longer a badge of virtue. Choicemakers work with God in creating a soul-satisfying life for themselves. You have to say *yes* to give life a try.

As a Protestant minister and woman, no one knows better than I do how taboo it feels to talk about taking risks and making decisions about how you want to live your life. Everything I've learned about what it means to be in ministry has emphasized the importance of surrendering your ambitions and will to God. And, of course, growing up female means that I've had ample lessons on how to coil your dreams and desires around the ankles of whatever man (or men) God sends into your life. As far as both teachings go, the self is the enemy. Small wonder that the ministry is filled with clergywomen who consider it ungodly to even think of giving up on relationships that show no sign of mending and feel it impossible to leave parishes where for years their gifts have been overlooked. The thought that they might have some choice in the matter sounds sacrilegious. But the lesson of the Garden of Eden was not that choosing for yourself is a sin. If anything the lesson was quite the opposite: sin is relying upon others to choose for you (Eve let the snake choose for her, and Adam permitted Eve's choice to be his choice). Owning up to your responsibility to make decisions and to being willing to accept the consequences of our choices is what it means to be alive ("a living soul" is the way the writer in Genesis 2:7 puts it).

You make some choices. I chose to teach, write, and be a minister just as much as teaching, writing, and the ministry chose me. I chose to give up my career as a stock-broker twenty-five years ago to pursue writing, which by some people's estimation, was a colossal mistake on my part since I never finished the novel I was writing, but I've never regretted a moment of it. I chose to put aside writing my Great American Novel to go to seminary and pursue full-time ministry, which I promptly changed my mind about when it became clear in my denomination that I could never hope as a woman to be assigned a church large enough to afford to pay me a full-time salary. I enrolled in a Ph.D. program after finishing seminary because I decided that since my prospects in the church were limited because I was a woman, I would go back, get a degree, and teach and change the church by teaching ministers and future leaders in the church. After twenty-five years of watching the church undergo changes in some of its attitudes about women (with little to no assistance from me, despite my youthful arrogant ambitions), witnessing firsthand God pruning me and fitting me for this and that opportunity, and finally reaching a place in my career when I don't feel split at the root, I can now float back and forth among all three professions monthly and yearly, never feeling welcome or rooted in any profession. Living on the edge of three professions is a way of life on one level I chose years ago, and on another level, I couldn't have prevented myself from choosing had I wished to. I am reminded of something Madam C. J. Walker, hair care specialist and first black woman millionaire back in the thirties, once said at a business luncheon in 1912:

I am a woman who came from the cotton fields of the South. From there I was promoted to the washtub. From there I was promoted to the cook kitchen. And from there I promoted myself into the business of manufacturing hair goods and preparations . . . I have built my own factory on my own ground.

But what if the path you're about to take leads you off the beaten path and falls outside the norm of what others deem acceptable? Didn't the Shulammite deserve the beating she got from the city guards (5:7)? After all, what business did she have roaming the streets at night in search of some man? Women don't pursue men; they sit back and wait to be pursued. Then there's the matter of her initiating intimacy, taking off in the middle of day to romp with her sweetheart, and openly sharing her fantasies with the public? Isn't such frankness and aggressiveness in women unfeminine? Isn't she guilty of acting the harlot? Isn't that what religion is for, to set up some guidelines for helping to protect us from ourselves?

Here is where we come to one of those pivotal forks in the road. We find ourselves having to decide on the norms, values, and attitudes that have been handed down to us for centuries—norms, values, and attitudes that probably reflect more our culture's views toward women than they do God's expectations of the female sex. The fact is that there have always been women and men who have refused to live their lives according to conventional norms. But the punishments for not doing so have not been meted out equally. While audiences are apt to respond with surprise, curiosity, and even a bit of admiration when men challenge the status quo, the same behavior in a woman is likely to evoke horror, revulsion, and ready indignation. How dare she? Who does she think she is? Get back in line. Men who do things their own way, who buck the system and play by their own rules, become the stuff of folk tales and go on to become cultural icons. Patrick Henry, Jesse James, Nat Turner, Toussaint Louverture, Malcolm X. Folks brand them rebels and outlaws, but a hint of admiration comes with the label.

Women who buck the system do not fare so luckily. They are likely to be labeled as pushy, hard, bossy, a witch, sapphire, jezebel, tramp, feminist, or other terms that are meant to raise questions about their sexual orientation. Unsurprisingly, name calling has always been a pretty effective weapon for making women get back in line. It's called baiting. Bait is what someone hurls at you—a comment, a label, an offer to do something—when they want to make you behave in a way they want you to and not in the way you've set as your focus. When the bait causes a shift in your equilibrium—you feel hurt, embarrassed, angry, or afraid—then you've taken the bait. No one wants to be branded a sapphire or tramp for having a mind of her own, but every woman who does have a mind of her own had better be prepared to be called these things, and worse, if she's going to choose a different path. You have to learn how to focus your energies and intelligence on what you want, and not allow your behavior to be determined by the bait that's been thrown in your direction. Keep this in mind: baiting is a power play designed to keep you in your place.

Perhaps this explains why we've heard few sermons about the Shulammite and the poetry in Song of Solomon preached from our pulpits. No one knows what to make of a stubborn, hardheaded woman who's not afraid to decide for herself what she wants. She refuses to bend to custom that likes to portray women as indecisive and unstable. There's always been a place for headstrong men who march to a different rhythm. They go on to become politicians, preachers, and power brokers. But where to put headstrong women? The church historically has had no office or position to offer women who challenged the status quo. Such women had to look elsewhere for role models on how to live life as a choicemaker.

For example, when the time came for an ex-slave named Sojourner Truth to decide whether she was going to remain silent or take a stand on women's right to vote, she drew strength from biblical women to defend her beliefs. She drew on the example of Eve and Mary to argue that while it's true that Christ didn't come to the world as a woman (which was the opponent's argument), he sure came into the world *through* a woman (without the assistance of any mortal man, thank you very much); and if the first woman God ever made was strong enough to turn the world upside down, then women armed with the vote ought to be able to turn it right side up again.

We have no way of knowing who the Shulammite

looked to for inspiration and example as she was growing up. Girls take their cues from the women around them when trying to figure out appropriate and inappropriate feminine behavior. Perhaps her mother was her inspiration. After all, her mother is referenced three times in the tiny book (6:9; 8:1, 2), which may say something about the older woman's influence upon her daughter. But we can't be sure. There's also the chance that she grew up hearing the legends of Deborah, Esther, and the Queen of Sheba, and other Hebrew women who changed the course of her people's history. I believe it was the English writer Virginia Woolf who said that women think back through their mothers. Sometimes mothers fade from the scene too soon, too suddenly, too completely, without leaving their daughters any hint of a notion of how to choose differently for themselves. More than twenty-five years of journals will be left behind as something of a compass for my own daughter should she be interested in reading them when she grows old enough to wonder whether, and how, it's possible as a woman not to cave in when the time comes to choose between a full life of her own making and a partial promise that someone else offers her.

Sniffing out the scent of a woman's story in the Bible is no easy task for those of us who have devoted our lives to helping women find stories worth passing on to their daughters. There's rarely enough in the Bible to go on: a verse here, a couple of verses there, a paragraph here, a mention there; a spoken word or two, nameless and voiceless mostly. Stories about women in the Bible are upon closer inspection rarely stories in the Bible about women. More often they are stories about men where women are supporting actresses, stock characters, literary asides, or stick figures who are brought in from outside to legitimate, show up, or act as a catalyst for the man or men who are invariably the main characters of the drama. Song of Solomon stands out as the only biblical book in which a woman's voice predominates. Her beloved speaks up in the book, but his voice is overshadowed by hers. As a result, the Shulammite offers a rare glimpse into a woman who stands as a role model of a bold, assertive, uninhibited, spirited woman who decides what she wants and goes after it. For those looking for biblical models of an assertive woman, the Shulammite is an ideal candidate. Not enough biographical detail is supplied to answer all our questions about her. But there's enough here to let us know that choices have consequences, and whenever a woman decides to follow a different course from the one others deem appropriate, she's bound to encounter criticism and obstruction.

One of the most important lessons to be learned if you're going to be a choicemaker is that every obstacle is not a sign from God that you should turn around and go back to doing what you were doing.

My experience is that women are quick to view pain and frustration as reasons to quit doing whatever they are doing. "My body was so sore after exercising that I decided against going back to that aerobics class." Never mind that you're only a week into the class after decades of being physically inactive. "We were so happy in the beginning of the marriage. But now that we're having all these problems, I'm beginning to wonder whether God is trying to tell me that I made a mistake." What does this say about your expectation of marriage? "I pray, but I don't feel that my prayers are being heard by God." Translation: Prayer should be easy; if I don't feel it, then it can't be real; and growing spiritually shouldn't be something I have to work at. Wrong. Wrong. Wrong. You will never become the woman you want to become until you learn how not to disintegrate in the face of difficulty, learn how to stay focused despite whatever difficulties that come your way, and learn how to disarm difficult people. It's easy to bloom when you live and work in climate-controlled environments. But until you figure out how to flourish and blossom even in the most intemperate conditions, your desires will forever remain at the level of desires.

Until more biographies of women ministers are written, those of us in ministry will have to piece scripts together where we can find them. In my ongoing search for role models and stories against which I might gauge my life, I have had to content myself with what I've been able to piece together about women in the music industry. Close friends know how much I love the music of female jazz singers. I listen to instrumental jazz and have been known to stop in my tracks at the sound of Joe Williams, Mel Tormé, or Billy Eckstine crooning on the radio. But when I'm banging out a book, a speech, a class lecture, or a sermon on my computer, I need the gutsy voices of women such as Sarah Vaughan, Shirley Horne, Ella Fitzgerald, Dinah Washington, Billie Holiday, Betty Carter, and others echoing in the background. Why female jazz singers? When I hear Ella, Sarah, or Dinah and others testifying about "the love that got away," about "feeling like a motherless child," or confessing "I love you, Porgy," or singing tauntingly to "cry me a river," I know that I am listening to women who have survived calamity and have lived to sing about it. There are sure to be those who will find it taboo for a Christian inspirational writer to admit that jazz singers are her inspiration. But wisdom, inspiration, and insight can come from many quarters. Indeed the writer of Proverbs 1:20 makes it clear that wisdom can be gotten readily from many different quarters if you're willing to pay attention: "*Wisdom cries out in the street; in the squares she raises her voice. At the busiest corner she cries out; at the entrance of the city gates she speaks.* My experience is that God uses a myriad of ways and a whole spectrum of experiences in which to communicate to us.

I am admittedly drawn to choicemakers, regardless of their profession. Choicemakers decide on a course and, despite the hardships, do not look back. There are no guarantees. There is only the chance to learn, grow, and follow your dreams. As a choicemaker, you learn to pause to sort out your priorities and motives, and the potential of a situation. You have to think through what your choices are, consider what choices will cost you emotionally, predict as best you can where the decision might lead you, and figure out intuitively what matters most to you. On the basis of who you are and what you know, you must make a decision about which path to take. When a woman is young, say, in her twenties, she's apt to minimize and renounce her strength because she fears that she'll miss out on finding a mate and starting a family if she exhibits all of her strength and intelligence. Minimizing your strength is easy when you are, like most, clueless about who you are and what you're capable of. A woman in her thirties, on the other hand, has had an opportunity to learn a few things about herself and is less likely to denounce her strength, though she stands ready to tell herself many times that she's perfectly willing (and able) to fold it up and tuck it away if Mr. Right comes along, offering his arm, thereby making it unnecessary for her to flex her muscles. "When Sleeping Beauty wakes up," writes the poet Maxine Kumin, "she's likely to be 50 years old." That's just about the time when a woman cares little about what others think and becomes almost obsessed with exercising more control over her own life.

Finally, God offers every one of us choices, decisions, the opportunity to learn and grow from our experiences, and the invitation to work with God in shaping who we will become. Your life will have its share of failures and of unchosen circumstances, for certain, but it is not just what happens to us that shapes us, but what happens inside us that makes all the difference. We can and do survive deprivation, loss, a broken heart, assault, illness, and having to start over because we learn how to separate what's happening to us from the essence of who we are. "I made a bad decision by letting my guard down and allowing my last boyfriend into my life. But that doesn't make me a stupid woman. I just made a bad decision." "My mother was an alcoholic who couldn't be counted on to protect me when I was growing up, but there's nothing to keep me from making different choices and being a better mother to my children." "I have breast cancer, but that doesn't mean I'm being punished by God for something from my past." "I am divorced, not unlovable."

There is in every woman the potential to be the heroine, not the victim, in her own journey. You become a heroine by refusing to beat up on yourself for mistakes you made in the past and by refusing to see choices as an ambush and opportunity for failure. Distinguishing real love from the fantasy of being rescued, learning how to choose a course of action for yourself and seeing it out to its end, is what gets easier as you begin to accept that you are a choicemaker. It's one of those lessons many of us didn't learn until we were well into our forties because it took that long to unlearn old lessons, although it needn't take our daughters and their friends that long to learn now that they have us to tell them the truth. I wish there had been someone in my life when I was in my twenties honest enough to tell me the truth. Someone who might have prodded me to ask myself, "What if I, and I alone, am responsible for my happiness, my success, and my overall well-being?" I might have made some different choices sooner instead of later. How about you?

Reflections on Choices

As a choice maker you learn to pause to sort out your priorities and motives, and the potentialities of a situation. You have to think through what your choices are, consider what choices will cost you emotionally, predict as best you can where the decision might lead you, and figure out intuitively what matters most to you. Such is the main point of this chapter.

1. How much time do you spend anguishing over choices? How much time do you spend beating up on yourself about the choices you've made, or failed to make?

_____

_____

2. What innovative ideas have you had lately that excited you but didn't move you to act? Why did you fail to act on them?

_____

_____

3. Finish this sentence. So, I failed in the past to

_____

_____ .

But, thank God, today is a new day. There's still a chance I can _____

_____ .

4. Finish this sentence. Today I choose _____

_____ .

Inner Wisdom

"Different seasons in our lives call on different aspects of our personality."

*Y*our desire for a full and fulfilling life will force you to stop and regularly confer with your deepest self. These are the moments when you must assess what your spiritual and emotional reactions, as well as your intellectual reactions, are to what's taking place in your life. Conferring on a routine basis with your deepest self helps you to remain true to your values and sees to it that you stay in conversation with the things you hold sacred in your heart. Several times throughout the poetry, the Shulammite addresses "the daughters of Jerusalem," who serve as a springboard to her private reflections (2:1–7; 3:5; 8:4). The concerns the Jerusalem daughters themselves raise to the Shulammite about what she wants are the kinds of concerns a woman who is honest asks herself in her moments of meditation. The Jerusalem daughters, in the style of a Greek chorus, serve as interlocutors, voices of wisdom, who raise questions at critical points in the book, recalling key ideas, anticipating new insights, always goading the Shulammite to think about what she's doing and what she's really after in pursuing the relationship with the shepherd. *"Who is your beloved more than others, O fairest among women?"* they ask in 5:9. *"Where has your beloved gone?"* they inquire in 6:1. *"Turn around, turn around, O Shulammite. Turn around, turn around, return, that we may look upon you. What is there to see in the Shulammite . . .?"* they ask in 6:13. (Another way to understand this last verse is, "Come inside, O Shulammite, for a little while and listen to your own spirit, pray, and cease with all the frenetic activity.")

Exactly who the daughters of Jerusalem are is not clear in the poetry. Are they real or imagined? Are they friends who have mixed emotions about the relationship unfolding before them? Are they spectators with no vested interest in the Shulammite's happiness who can't see what all the fuss is about? Are they empathetic or disdainful of the courtship? Are they a literary creation of the poet, meant to serve as the voice of the audience? How many of them are there? The poet doesn't say. She leaves it to our imagination to figure all this out on our own. I like to think of the Jerusalem daughters as both real and imagined friends of the Shulammite. They represent the very tangible and real circle of friends every woman needs in her life who add deep, rich texture to her life. Having a circle of friends to draw on and to relate to, instead of just one friend, allows you to be demanding of your friendships. No one friend has to be everything to you. My best friend in fourth grade was Deborah, in seventh grade Anna, in eleventh grade Cynthia. Each relationship was intense and stormy. We didn't know how to give each other permission to be friends with other people. We thought it was a betrayal to have two best friends simultaneously. Which explains why I felt crushed when Deborah started spending time with Valerie while still claiming to be my friend. But best friend doesn't have to mean the friend you love the most. Your best friend is that someone with whom you have a deep rapport as it relates to some very special areas of your life. But no one person can possibly be everything to you.

Every woman should have different friends for the many different parts of herself and for the many different occasions in her life. We each have an inner core where our deepest feelings, needs, and beliefs are buried, and we typically have an inner circle of friends with whom we share our inner core of feelings and needs. If you want a real lesson in the passage of time, try getting together with a friend you haven't seen in ten, twenty, or thirty years. It's a wonderful way to find out just how much you've changed or not changed. It took Barbara, whom I'd not spoken heart to heart with in years, to remind me of the girl I was in my twenties. We ran into each other in New York City one summer after more than twenty years had passed. "You've always insisted upon doing things exactly the way you wanted, Renita," she said rather casually as she reached for her iced tea. I was speechless. Funny, that's not how I remember the twenty-something me. I remember feeling as if I had no choice but to follow the path I had because I didn't have the good fortune of a husband, children, stability, income, and respectability like Barbara and other friends I had at the time. Which one of us is right, I sat there wondering. Both of us, I suppose.

Of my six closest friends today, no two are the same. Each one has the ability to bring the outside world to me in different ways when I'm wrestling with a problem. More important, each one lets me display a different side of my personality when I'm in her presence. The number of friends we have isn't as important as the diversity of the friendships. A range of friends—from colleagues to neighbors, from buddies to prayer partners—can meet a range of needs we have. There's no better time to have a wide circle of friends to draw from than when, like the Shulammite, you find yourself going through a storm. It sure helps to know that Elaine will check on you regularly, Jessica will be your intercessory prayer partner, Claudette and Cynthia will allow you to speak your angriest thoughts without judgment, and JoAnn will listen understandingly to your description of your pain because she's been there. I am grateful for friends whom I've known and who have known me for ten, twenty, and in some cases almost thirty years. Every woman needs her own Jerusalem daughters—true, genuine friends who as soul mates, prayer partners, playmates, and accounta-bility partners will encircle her like a life raft—when one too many waves have crashed in on her and left her flailing and struggling to stay afloat.

What about those of you who complain that you don't have friends? Sometimes you have to give yourself what you wish you could get from others. It's possible that the Jerusalem daughters weren't real women after all. They just may have been the imaginary friends a woman car-ries around within her to survive, the kind of intuitive voices that live inside all of us that beckon us to trust our gut, be careful, go for it, or think again. In Song of Solomon the Jerusalem daughters serve a literary func-tion as the conscience and sounding board for the Shu-lammite's musing and decision making. Inside you and me, they are our sacred inner committee, the multiple sides of ourselves, who each has a role and a value.

The term *daughters of Jerusalem* is a title used by prophets and poets throughout the Old Testament to refer metaphorically to the villages or towns surrounding Jerusalem that functioned as fortified military outposts (Isaiah 37:22; Zephaniah 3:14; Zechariah 9:9). Invaders had to pass through and subdue each fortified outpost if they wanted to reach Jerusalem, the capital city, and attack it. In the poetry of Song of Solomon, the Jerusalem daughters are the collective wisdom of the Shulammite that rise up to steady her and keep her clear about what's happening. At critical points in the poem, they raise the sorts of questions the Shulammite, and every woman in love, surely asked herself, proving just how complex and powerful love really is. We ask ourselves, *"Exactly who is this man, and what makes him so different from others?"* or *"When he's away from me, how do I know I can trust him?"* or *"What kind of love is this that it has me torn in so many different directions?"* Once smitten, we can't help, despite our misgivings, to love anyway. It is in the nature of love, of course, that we're able to brush aside our questions and justify our feelings. And that's just what the Shulammite does to the questions raised by the Jerusalem daughters. But that doesn't stop the Jerusalem daughters from asking the questions that they do. They represent her God-given instincts. The Shulammite is to be commended for at least pausing long enough to honor their questions, even if in the end she goes about her merry way and falls in love. Think of it like this: Within you is a committee of women who represent your collective wisdom, each of whom represents an insight or side of you that is the result of the experiences you've had over the years. You can ignore them, but you can't altogether silence them either.

Women are notorious for going against what we know inside and trying to make bad relationships work. We remain friends with people who deplete us. We do things that go against our basic instincts and feelings as children of God. Worst of all, we learn as girls and women to put up with chronic crisis and conflict. Our lives and relationships are one drama after another. Nonetheless, every woman has a committee of women living inside her that can help her in times of crisis. The members of your internal committee represent different parts of yourself, competing sides of your personality, a multiplicity of inner voices clamoring for expression. The chair of the committee is the you who's eager for a full life but who doesn't know where to begin. How are you supposed to negotiate the clamoring voices within? "I keep a journal," a writer once told me, "in order to stay in conversation with the many women who live inside me." That's as good advice as any on the wisdom of journaling. Get to know the women who make up your internal committee by writing about each one of them. Journaling helps you get to know the different sides of yourself.

Unfortunately, some women never quite learn how to preside over or reconcile the different women who exist inside them. They never learn that we are all a mass of inner conflicts and divided loyalties. To them, an inner chorus of voices is a sign of their mental and spiritual weakness, their failure at being strong women of faith who act out of the strength of a supposedly undivided self. No one has ever told them that there's no such thing as being single-minded and having one side to your personality. Human beings are far more complex than that. They have to be. After all, different situations call for different sides of ourselves. More important, different seasons in our lives call on different aspects of our personality.

Pausing to caucus with the women who make up you,

therefore, is not a sign of faithlessness, indecisiveness, or worse, mental defect. We all carry around within our heads voices that vie with one another about what's best for us. Each voice has value and a role to play in your life. Taking time out to confer within is good for the soul. The questions each voice raises are derived from your goodly instincts, and they are designed to ask *the* precise psychological question that often opens up secret doors within. It's only by listening to the questions of your conscience that you discover the stuff that you don't know that you know. Asking the proper question is the central action to transforming your life, reinventing yourself, shaking you out of denial, waking up from the deep sleep you're in. Jesus asked the man at the pool of Bethsaida, "Do you want to be healed?" On the face of it, what a dumb question to ask someone who's been crippled for much of his life. But maybe it isn't such a dumb question when you think about all the benefits that come with playing the role of victim. Are you prepared to stand on your own two feet and turn back in the welfare checks you've collected over the years, return the handouts you've received, and give up the special attention you've come to enjoy? Questions that pop up in your mind when you're faced with a decision cause both mind and soul to germinate. If there's a secret something about this person, something forbidden about the whole matter, a side of all of this that you yourself don't want to look at but should, it needs to be looked at. It's important to get away and take time to hear yourself (your *selves*, I should say) think. Pay attention to the questions. Call time-out, go inward, and call for a committee meeting. Journaling is one way to get at what you're thinking. Talking out loud to yourself is another way to let each woman have her say. Therapy is another viable option.

Take, for example, having to make a major decision about a job opportunity that has come along. Of course, we are taught to admire the woman who seems to know what she wants and goes after it. But you find yourself conflicted about which direction to take. You're torn by the competing loyalties. A chorus of persistent little voices rises up inside, one expressing fear about traipsing off into unknown territory, another warning you against being overly confident about your chances to do the job, another whispering that you're better off where you are. Those are the so-called negative voices, the supposedly nasty little saboteurs inside all of us that, if not balanced by a subcommittee of more daring, self-confident voices, subvert, derail, and undermine our aspirations. The sup-posedly positive voices are the ones that goad us to try new things, take chances, throw caution to the wind, live a little, and exercise more faith in God and in our-selves. Suppress your doubts and ignore your fears, the popular pundits advise. But it's not as simple as all that. The woman who acts in a way that's true to herself and in her own best interests is the woman who has learned how to call an inner committee meeting and to preside over all the members of her committee, hear each woman out, weigh the advice of each, and then act in the best interest of her goals and values. The women within represent the sum of all the experiences, emotions, and wisdom you've garnered over the years, all of which go into making you the wonderfully complex, passionate, and captivating woman that you are.

When you're young, you're apt to feel anxious about your decisions. You lack clarity about your own ambitions and dreams, and frequently need the advice and approval of others (outside you) to serve as your compass. But as you get older, you gain more confidence as you begin to trust your own internal wisdom. You learn the secret to chairing the committee and not censoring the voices. They represent you, the glorious and less-than-glorious parts of yourself. They balance you out. You learn to listen to your feelings and impulses, caucus with your soul, hear yourself think, and search your heart. And even if you decide incorrectly, it's not the end of the world, the wise woman discovers. You learn and reconvene the committee. There's bound to be something (or someone) else within that you can draw from to rebuild upon.

Through journaling I've managed to identify at least five different women who make up my inner committee, and I have given a name to each.

There's Faustina, my critic. Nothing is good enough for her. She's never satisfied. No book or article I write is ever ready to be seen by the public, according to her. No sermon I preached was good enough. There was always something that just wasn't right. She's critical of the way my body looks as I age. She insists upon excellence, and I appreciate her for that; but if I'm not careful, she will silence me before anyone else has a chance to do so.

There's the bully within, whom I've labeled Shayshay. She refuses to take no for an answer. She's my hard taskmaster. She drives me to exhaustion and hysteria with her will to succeed and win, and her determination to crush anything and anyone who gets in the way of what she wants. She refuses to be intimidated. In fact, she hates for anyone to try to intimidate her. By the way, did I mention that Shayshay remembers every hurt and wrong anyone has ever inflicted on me? She is bent upon proving my naysayers wrong.

Neecie is forever apprehensive about trying new things. She sees ghosts and goblins around every corner, and cautions me against making a complete fool of myself. She's the first to remind me "I told you so" when making a fool of myself is just what I've done. No matter how much God blesses me, Neecie can't help looking for doom and disaster to strike at any moment. She teaches me caution, but she's wholly incapable of coming to my aid when trying to figure out how to get out of a jam.

Then there's Wanda the Wonderer, who's the antithesis of Neecie. Wanda is always seduced by the next adventure. She is easily distracted. She's the girl in me who's filled with wonder and curiosity. She loves trying new things. She loves a dare, and is elated to tackle new creative possibilities. She never allows herself to get bogged down with the big picture, the practical realities, the consequences of an action. Wanda always has big ideas, so don't bother her with practicalities.

At last, there's Inez the Intellectual. Inez is a brooder. She is a thinker. She prefers contemplation over action. She's not critical like Faustina or scared like Neecie. Inez just likes to think and think and think. She prefers books to people, sending e-mail over placing a phone call, and the solitude of her own thoughts over the push and pull of relationships. Give her time, and she'll figure out most things. But you must give her time. Of course, you'll be glad you did, if you can wait for her to make up her mind. When she's at her best, she is thoughtful and wise. If left unchecked, she's a procrastinator, and a moody one at that.

Westerners recoil from talk about the self as having different sides to it lest we appear divided and self-conflicted. Christian women shy away from talk about the self for fear of coming across as self-absorbed and selfish. But the depiction of the Jerusalem daughters in Song of Solomon reminds us that there are different sides of our personalities and competing voices that we all carry around in our hearts. Call them instinct. Call them intuition. Call them your inner committee. Listening for and to God often involves "trusting that still small voice(s) within." How do you do that? you ask. Trust your instincts. Respect your feelings. Give yourself credit for knowing some things. Listen to your life. Close the door. Take time to hear yourself think. Pray. Listen to your body. Don't allow yourself to be pressured into replying when you feel you need more time. Give yourself time to get back to the person with an answer. Don't talk your-self into liking someone you don't like, or trusting someone you don't trust. Be cordial, but keep your distance. There are things we know that we don't even know that we know. Failure to honor the voices within is a sure way to make you dependent on others for advice and wisdom. I wish someone had told me this years ago at the one and only time in my life when I thought seriously about taking my own life. I couldn't turn off the voices that were screaming back and forth in my head telling me what to do. Instead of learning how to chair the committee and draw on the wisdom of the voices gathered around the table, I huddled in the dark and wept. I dreamed of ways to quiet everyone, including me.

Finally, people often ask me, as a writer, where the courage to pursue my desires comes from. Why God, of course. More pointedly it comes from a place within us where all the wisdom we've gained over the years is stored. It's a place where lessons learned, insights gained, and dreams dreamed are stored for safekeeping. In that sacred place and around that sacred table sits God, who waits to help us put the pieces of the puzzle together. With growing up, growing older, and growing wiser comes learning how to dive deep inside yourself to get what you need from yourself—and from God. All the information you need to do what you need to do is there waiting for you. It's a matter of learning how to break the surface, diving deep within, and sitting still long enough to hear what emerges.

I've shared with you my five secret selves. What are yours? Take a blank sheet of paper, and list, name, and describe your inner committee of secret selves. Get acquainted with them. Listen to what each one has to say. Thank her for her perspective. Introduce her to the other women on the committee so she will know that she has to learn how to coexist and collaborate with other women with equally important perspectives to share about the choices you make and the direction you take.

Reflections on Inner Wisdom

If making and keeping friends is difficult for you, this chapter may cause you some discomfort. But don't give up on yourself or on the chapter. Listen with your soul. Perhaps the Spirit is speaking to you. *We each have an inner core where our deepest feelings, needs, and beliefs are buried, and we typically have an inner circle of friends with whom we share our inner core of feelings and needs.*

1. How has friendship become more or less important in your life in recent years? Why has its value changed?

_____

_____

_____

2. Have you ever had a friendship end because of conflict? Do you now know ways to handle that conflict that might have saved that friendship?

_____

_____

_____

3. Name those whom you count as your closest friends. What does each person bring to your life? Have you told them? Tell them.

_____

_____

_____

4. How do you know when you've gone against your own best judgment and made a decision that transgresses who you are?

_____

_____

_____

5. What ritual have you set up for spending time with yourself, for conferring with the Spirit, for listening to that still small voice within?

_____

_____

_____

Danger

❦

"Come what may, I will survive."

Your desire for a full and fulfilling life will eventually place you at odds with forces, both internal and external, that are aligned against your desire to thrive. You will have to gather all the strength available to you to face headlong this resistance, which in most instances wants nothing less than to plunder your soul. It's one of the most painful moments in your life. For all our talk about women honoring their desires and following them, we all know that to grow up female is to grow up constantly on guard against predators who prey on the vulnerable people in our society, namely women and children. Mothers of daughters are especially attuned to a paradox that, in truth, is at the heart of this book: You look down lovingly at the tender young maiden whom God has entrusted in your care to raise, and you want to raise her to be fearless, to take risks, and to make her own choices. But at what cost, you ask yourself. You know that as soon as she steps outside what society has deemed the safety zone for "good girls," there will be those who want nothing more than to snatch her into the underworld. "What was she doing out that late anyway?" "Why was she riding her bike alone on the street?" "She shouldn't have been wearing such provocative clothes." "Who does she think she is anyway?" "She should have kept her mouth shut." "That explains why she isn't married." It's easier to blame the victim than it is to stop the offender. Violence against women and girls is too pervasive across the world for us to be satisfied with simplistic answers.

As much as we'd like to focus on the playful and seductive nature of the poetry in Song of Solomon, to overlook the hint of shadow and danger embedded in the heroine's story is to ignore the truth about what it means to grow up female. In a story like Song of Solomon, where the ambience is frolicsome and love is in the air, we have to ask ourselves what we are to make of the heroine's beating by the city guards in 5:7. Why does the Shulammite drop this bit of menace on us in an otherwise exuberant book about love? One way to see it is as part of the book's larger tale of a romance impeded by circumstances, and the lengths to which the heroine goes to be united with the object of her love. Audiences are asked to understand the innocence of the woman and man's love and to empathize with the absurdity of the obstacles and frustrations they are forced to endure to be together. After all, impediments and obstructions are common devices in romance fiction to heighten drama. Searching and finding; now you see him, now you don't; now she has him, now she doesn't; ridicule by family; the questions and skepticism of onlookers; attacks by perfect strangers (i.e., sentinels)—these are the devices a poet uses to draw out romance and to leave audiences on edge wondering about the fate of the love affair. This is one explanation for including the verse about the attack the heroine endures in Song of Solomon 5:7.

But a poet is only as convincing as she is able to make her story mirror real life. Could it be that the Shulammite wants to warn us as women against letting negative, evil, malevolent forces around us extinguish our will to live and to be whole? But to be on guard against them, you must first recognize that they are there. We are all likely to overlook the violence mentioned in 5:7 and not give it very much attention. We expect women who traipse through the streets at night, even for good reasons, to encounter danger. Our heroine's beating doesn't surprise us. We read over it. And that's precisely my point. We expect danger. We live with danger as women. But we are not outraged by it. We've become so accustomed to images of women beaten, raped, abducted, and bludgeoned to death in the media that our senses have grown dulled to their senselessness and implications.

"Aren't you being hard on men?" certain women are wont to ask when you bring up the matter of violence against women. Christian women especially are quick to flinch when the topic comes up. "Why don't you just focus on the good news that Jesus Christ brings into women's lives and stop harping on all this talk about violence against women, which is only designed to keep us fearful and suspicious of the men God sends into our lives?" was how it was put to me in an e-mail by a disgruntled reader who'd read an article I'd written on violence. These are the women who refuse to consider the possibility that our failure to question and challenge widely held religious beliefs about women's submission and obedience might just be contributing to our culture's deadly confusion of love and romance with domination and control. They don't get it:

- That every nine seconds a woman is battered (according to a 1991 study conducted by the U.S. Justice Department).
- That two-thirds of these attacks are committed by someone the victim knew, such as a husband, a boyfriend, another family member, or an acquaintance—a much higher figure than for men.
- That the Justice Department's Bureau of Justice Statistics found approximately 2.5 million of the nation's 107 million females twelve years old and older were raped, robbed, or assaulted in a typical year, or were the victim of a threat or an attempt to commit such a crime.

- That in the United States, a woman is more likely to be assaulted, injured, raped, or killed by a male partner than any other assailant.

- That wife-beating results in more injuries that require medical treatment than rape, auto accidents, and muggings combined.

- That in a study of females killed by intimate partners between 1980 and 1982, it was found that the majority of women killed were married (57.7%). Girlfriends were the next highest percentage (24.5%), followed by common-law wives (8%), ex-wives (4.89%), and friends (4.675%).

- That battering accounts for 25% of female suicide attempts per year.

Women who are afraid we're bashing men when we speak out against women's victimization by violence don't seem to get the fact that there is a difference between taking a stand against this or that man (which I am not advocating) and taking a stand against anyone or any system that insists that battering you, humiliating you, stifling you, belittling you, and silencing you as a woman—emotionally, mentally, physically, or spiritually—even in the name of love is a God-given prerogative. We can never hope to experience the repentance, forgiveness, and reconciliation that we all look forward to in our faith until we are prepared to give both victims and perpetrators permission to talk openly about the ways in which we have all been wounded by misguided teachings, by bad (though well-meaning) theology, by unreasonable cultural expectations thrust on us as women and men, and by some rather wrongheaded notions we have about what love and intimacy entails.

This week, as I write this chapter on desire and danger, stories of girls abducted from their homes are in the media. Every mother of a daughter is clutching her breast in fear these days. We've ordered our daughters inside, locked the doors, and pulled down the shades. No more riding her bike on the street. No more playing outside with her best friend next door. No more taking the car out at night to meet a friend. No more giving in when she protests that you're old-fashioned to think her pants are too tight. We are scared for our daughters and goddaughters. We are reminded how mean the world can be to females and struggle to find a way to pass this information along to them without dampening their enthusiasm for life. We are afraid for them and for ourselves. Our sons are not safe either. But the violence against women and girls *feels* different to me, at least. Perhaps because I'm female. Perhaps because it *is* different. If spirituality does anything for you, it ought to make you face the truth so that you can get the clarity you need to make connections. Once you get clarity, it ought to give you the courage as a thinking woman of faith to address the issues you've identified. It's time for women of faith to take a stand against violence against women and girls. As Audre Lorde the poet reminds us in one of her essays,

"My silences did not protect me. Your silence will not protect you."

Jesus said, "You shall know the truth, and the truth shall set you free." What he didn't say, which I've learned the hard way, is that one reason we would rather not face the truth, despite its promise of freedom, is because the truth hurts. It hurts to face the fact that violence against women and girls is not just the violence we come to expect in a violent culture. These are crimes by males against females in many cases *because* they are females. Breaking into a home in the middle of the night and abducting a teenage girl from her bedroom and holding her hostage for nine months as one's wife or even as one's daughter is a crime prompted by the fact that she's female. Snatching five-, six-, seven-year-old girls from their front yards where they were playing, then raping and strangling them, and dumping their young bodies in the woods are crimes against girls because they are girls (not exclusively against girls, mind you, but such crimes happen around the globe daily against girl children with alarming frequency).

Some days I read the news about another woman murdered by her husband or another girl snatched from her home, I watch another woman beaten up on one of my favorite cop shows and see another teenage girl compete for the chance on a music video to be photographed in a humiliating pose with a rap singer, and I find myself asking God whether there is a war against women that I'm just waking up to? You don't have to agree that there's an all-out conspiracy against women, but you should be able to agree as a woman that something is wrong in the way in which our society views women and girls. Even being a "good girl" does not ensure your survival. Bad things can and do happen to good girls. It's possible to wake up one day and discover that you're in love with a man who hates women. Then there are the anonymous phone calls and unsigned harassing letters threatening us with what will be done to us if we don't back down, get back in line, or keep silent. And then there are the daily put-downs, insults, sexist jokes, sarcastic remarks, and inappropriate touching that we endure, the intended or unintended result of which is to hack away at our confidence and self-esteem. It takes drawing on all the resources God has given you to be able to discern when you're in the presence of a jerk and someone just plain obnoxious, or when something or someone truly menacing is afoot. Don't allow yourself to be so caught up in your fantasies that you're completely blind to the danger around you, the Shulammite warns.

Stories that describe the rape and plunder of women are not for the fainthearted. The Bible is replete with such stories. But few of us want to look at them closely. We are afraid because these stories never have a happy ending, not really. They are just *there* for us to muddle through their meaning: the rape of Dinah, the daughter of Leah and Jacob in Genesis 34, and of Tamar, the daughter of King David in 2 Samuel 13; the butchered concubine in Judges 19; Gomer, the abused wife in

Hosea 1–3; the sexually ravaged woman in Ezekiel 16 and 23; and the woman caught in adultery in John 8, just to name a few. We mustn't overlook these stories just so we can keep up our belief in the notion that bad things happen only to bad people, or that women are safe as long as they keep to the script that's been handed down to them, or that evil can be kept at bay simply by praying it away. It doesn't happen that way, not always, and not for everybody. Not enough is written or said to those of us who are women of faith about the evil and dangers that align themselves against us simply because we are women. Not enough intelligent things have been written or said anyway. But the whole point of the story of the assault against the Shulammite, and the other stories of terror that I've listed above, is to make us face what we don't want to face.

In almost every case in the Bible, the assault is against a high-spirited woman who is set upon a course of action she has decided for herself. The Shulammite is out searching the streets for her beloved. Dinah has left the safety of her father's compound for an outing with other women in her region (Genesis 34). The woman (allegedly) caught in adultery has defied custom by living in a common-law arrangement with a man (John 8:1–11). Violence is the penalty for each woman's defiance. We can see these stories then as a threat and warning to headstrong, high-spirited women who follow their own desires. Or we can see each story as an invitation when we get together in our book groups and study groups for us to ask deeper questions about such stories and the women we know who've shared their fate. The writers of these stories neither applaud nor condemn the violence, for if they did, perhaps we'd know what to do with the stories. Instead, they leave it to us readers to use our faith and good sense to figure out what must be done.

Life is full of unchosen circumstances, as I've mentioned elsewhere in this book, but there are always moments of decision, the "nodal points" that alter character and change the course of one's life. You and I may not always be able to prevent the tide of danger that lurks about to snuff out our spirit. But neither are we as defenseless as we are apt to believe. Two things bear keeping in mind. First, the story of violence in the Bible teaches us that there is a presence in the universe that preys upon women and girls and whose objective appears to be to frighten us to stay put, keep our desires to a minimum, and above all, keep quiet. Second, you can allow fear of such a force to make you live your life emotionally, spiritually, and psychologically crouching in a corner and unwilling to face what's there in the hopes of staving off any disaster directed at you. Or you can decide, "Come what may, I will survive." Which is not to be interpreted as a sort of resignation where you accept the fact that whatever happens is going to happen, and there's not much you can do about it. You can say, "Come what may, I will survive" as a woman facing danger headlong, refusing to let it leave her perpetually crouched and ducking from what her imagination sees.

In studies of women who have endured childhoods of abuse, cruelty, and deprivation, psychiatrists have found at least one striking difference between a survivor and a victim. Despite the appalling bruises she endured, the woman who survives and goes on to make a healthy life for herself usually had an inner core that she never surrendered to her abuser—no matter how much he (they) clamored to get at it and destroy it. Despite all the bad that was going on, a survivor has the uncanny ability to separate her outer circumstance from her inner reality. She does not escape a traumatic past unscathed; she has her share of scars. But she manages somehow to be able to maintain a sense of herself aside from what happened to her. Perhaps she had imaginary companions she talked to about what was going on. Perhaps she had an inner myth ("I'm really a princess, and these are all wicked people who want to abduct me") or an inner faith ("Jesus will save me") that kept her hope alive. Perhaps she had a fantasy life that she escaped to that made everything happening unreal ("This is not real, this is not happening to the real me") and kept her detached from the reality her tormentor wanted to inhabit. The point is that she found a way to escape into a world of her own making, nurse herself back, come out and hobble to somewhere where it was safe to look at what happened. The point is that survivors generally know to create their own myths and make up their own alternative universes.

The woman who is a perpetual victim, on the other hand, is likely to be the kind to give in to every threat hurled at her because she lacks an inner chamber at the core of her being where her most precious treasures are kept, namely her values and her truest self. She can't separate what is happening to her from what is happening within her. How quickly we are reminded when danger strikes that all we really have are the resources within to help pull us through: our faith, our wit, our intuition, our courage. It's probably safe to say that the psalmist didn't just have in mind our bowels, kidneys, and spleen only when he wrote, *"For it was you who fashioned my inward parts, who knit me together in my mother's womb"* (Psalm 139:13). Indeed God has fashioned a special place within us for us to retreat to and find refuge when the fiery darts are hurled at us along our journey. While we don't always have the luxury of avoiding danger, it is certainly possible to survive danger with your soul intact.

But the forces intent upon our undoing are not always external; some of them are internal. These are the subtler forces we have to wage against. Sometimes it's the dark, shadowy sides of our own personality that we have to be on guard against. They show up in the form of depression, low self-esteem, self-loathing, repressed anger, and holding on to old grudges. Convene a group of women friends together and ask how many within the group have had a long-term experience with at least one of these inner maladies while growing up female. As Christians we're tempted to speak of these maladies as demons because such negative feelings are so pervasively a part of women's testimonies about themselves and aren't easily gotten ridden of once they attach themselves to us. Not to mention the power they have potentially to drain you of the energies you need to live the healthy physical *and* emotional life Christ has promised you: "*I come that you might have life, and life more abundantly*" (John 10:10). But I've learned that the only way to begin to fight a demon is to confront a demon.

Let me give you an example of my own experience. While I think there's lots of wisdom to be gained from recording and studying one's dreams, I'm too lazy or too forgetful to follow this practice with any consistency. For one thing, I don't always remember to keep a dream journal on the nightstand to catch the memory of the dream before it gets away from me at the sound of the alarm, the television, or the chatter of a family member. It's true, however, that repeating to yourself before drifting off to sleep, "I *will* remember what I dream tonight" does work. I've tried it. But there's one recurring dream that I have that I don't need my dream journal to remind me of its frequency and intensity. It's my dark man dream.

Once or twice a month I am bolted awake in the middle of the night by my dream of a prowler outside wherever I am, most often my home, fumbling with the locks on the door so he can make his way in. Suddenly he's inside . . . I hear his footsteps . . . he's turning the corner to where I am . . . he's standing above me . . . I can see his outline (never his face) . . . I feel him reaching for me . . . I bolt up in bed. My heart is pounding; all the forms in my bedroom (the armoire, the clock on the wall, the television, the chair in the corner) are blurred and look menacing. Whether the man in my dreams is a rapist, a thug, a burglar, or even a friend who's come to tell me something, I don't know. I can't bear it; let the dream conclude. I'm too frightened. But I've learned something from my dreams. I no longer believe that my dark man dream is trying to warn me about some real prowler on the loose outside my house. I believe God can speak to me through dreams, but I also believe that dreams are messages from my unconscious that are sent to uncover a new layer of my conscious mind. More often, my dark man dream shows up when there's something I don't want to face. Something I'm avoiding. Something I would rather go away from. The predator comes to shake me to my senses and make me ask myself, "My Lord, what was that all about?," which often enough is just what my conscious mind needs to make me begin rummaging through some things to discover what I'm avoiding and bring it from the periphery to the center of my consciousness. Mind you, I didn't say that I am willing to deal with whatever it is. I just said that the startled feeling the dream leaves me with prompts me that it's time to look at it.

My dark man dream typically occurs whenever I've reached a block in my writing, when I have a dreaded speech to give, or when something is looming on the horizon that I've put off dealing with. His breaking into my psyche the way he does usually has one of two results. I may be roused to face the prowler and do something about the matter, or if I'm feeling rather weak and defenseless at the time (and I have many times), I sometimes give in to his scare tactics and cower and lie low, and put off taking him on until I feel stronger. Cowering to the fear is the way I dealt most often when I was younger. I didn't have the skills, courage, and wisdom to know how to fend off the depression and angst that filled me when I had one of my dark man dreams. I'm not so easily intimidated years later.

Every woman, especially every woman who is unconventional, every woman on the verge of some important spiritual, emotional, or psychological breakthrough, has some form of a recurring predatory dream: a stalker, a prowler, a mugger, someone running after her. The predator from within will either rouse you to action or frighten you into inaction. You will either become super-vigilant about doing what you've got to do to go to the next level of your life, or you will allow yourself to become intimidated by the unknown and what your predator wants you to believe is the undoable for a woman like yourself. The point here is that there are forces within and outside of us that will make us back down, if we let them. You must first confront these forces in order to conquer them. I still have dark man dreams. Not as often as I did in my thirties, but they still show up. That's because, perhaps, I'm still growing and evolving as a human being. I'm learning to make the dream a source of growth instead of a source of intimidation. I know what to say now when he shows up: "Okay, so you're back. Tell me what you have to tell me. And be gone."

The Shulammite would not be daunted. She recounts her beating at the hands of the city guards as she roamed the streets of Jerusalem in search of her beloved (5:7). They not only beat her, but take her cloak (which may be a veiled reference to a rape). In an earlier scene the sentinels did not interfere with her comings and goings (3:3), but this time she is not so lucky. They take advantage of her being out at night alone. A woman's worst nightmare is the price she pays for being a headstrong and high-spirited woman. Despite her attack, the Shulammite doesn't give up. She suffers terribly, but she gets back up, dusts herself off, and presses ahead. That's easier said than done. But you do start by telling yourself precisely that, again and again. Look at it this way: If your chances as a girl of being attacked aren't going to change, if you live in a society where protecting women and girls from the predatory fantasies of sick individuals is not a priority, if being a lady is no guarantee that you'll escape violence completely, then you may as well get back up, keep going, speak your mind, and follow your passions.

There's nothing more to lose. Silence hasn't protected you. Ask the Shulammite.

Finally, every woman proceeds on her own journey. On the journey she will confront tasks, obstacles, and dangers. She will have to decide how she will respond to what's thrown at her. By the next chapter of Song of Solomon our heroine has resumed her journey (6:11–12). What the sentinels did to her didn't change who she was on the inside. They saw a woman flouting custom. She saw herself as a high-spirited woman who knew what she wanted. She gathered her strength and struck out again when she was stronger and wiser. Healing and regaining one's strength and equilibrium after a trauma don't entail just returning to a former self in the past; it is the experience of growth and change that allows you to integrate all that has happened into a better, stronger, more clarified you. How you and I respond to and what we do after we've been wounded change us forever.

The woman who has been raised to be a lady and has bought into that notion will likely find parts of her personality stunted and silenced by all the change that's happened because ladies are taught to feign weakness and aren't likely to face headlong what's happening to them. But the woman who's decided to be an unconventional woman, a thinking woman of faith, has to be ready to endure the sounds of the Sirens in the rocks calling to her to shrivel up, back up, go no farther, turn back. Forces from within and without are sure to shake her to the core. She will taste fear. She will know disgust. She will feel shame. She will also taste victory. And if she's lucky, she will experience outrage. The kind of outrage that makes a woman wake up clarified. And if she remains true to the things God has stored away for her in her inner chamber, she will find the confidence that comes with learning how to transform anger into action and change. Ours is a journey of discovery and development, of integrating both the shadow and the light of our character into our whole, yet complex, personality.

Reflections on Danger

Each of us has been wounded in intentional and unintentional ways by society, by institutional religion, by those we love and who love us, and by complete strangers. *We can never hope to experience the repentance, forgiveness and reconciliation that we all look forward to in our faith until we are prepared to give both victims and perpetrators permission to talk openly about the ways in which we have all been wounded by misguided teachings, by bad (though well meaning) theology, by unreasonable cultural expectations thrust on us as women and men, and by some rather wrongheaded notions we have about what love and intimacy entail.*

1. Can you name some of the ways in which misguided teachings and unreasonable expectations have kept you stuck in unhealthy relationships and unable to see your potentialities as a woman of faith?

_____

_____

_____

_____

2. Name some women you know who lost their lives or suffered violently as a result of abusive relationships.

_____

_____

_____

3. What can be done to stem the tide of violence against women? What can we do to help younger women recognize violence in their own relationships and to respond appropriately?

_____

_____

_____

4. In what ways as women have we absorbed the message of our culture about violence and become abusers ourselves, perpetrating violence and evil against one another?

_____

_____

_____

Your Body

"You feel it in your bones."

Your desire for a full and fulfilling life has a chance quite possibly to end in satisfaction when you finally learn to tune into your body's needs. Sadly, you will have spent almost a lifetime learning how to trust your gut feeling about someone else's needs before you figure out how to trust that same inner wisdom to see what's going on with your own body. It would help if someone had taught us sooner how to give our bodies credit for their own innate wisdom. But no one did. We have had to learn the hard way through high blood pressure, migraines, tension, backaches, eating and sleep disorders, to name a few, to know when something is going wrong inside our bodies.

Of course, it's quite possible in a book about women's spirituality to discuss every part of a woman's being except her body. Somewhere in our collective past as human beings, we have been the victims of bad theology, plain and simple. We are not sinful, shameful human creatures who have somehow to earn the right to experience and know God on a spiritual level. It's quite possible, as others have pointed out, that we are at our inner core spiritual beings who have been put here on earth to have human experiences. If that's true, then it's not the body that communicates through the spirit, but the spirit that communicates with everything around it through the human body. What does all this mean? There are moments in your journey of growing into a passionate woman when you will know in your body, your gut, your insides that things are different, that you need to make some changes, that things are about to change. How will you know? You feel it in your bones. Perhaps it's not just with our spirits, but through our bodies that God communicates with us and we with God.

Let me use an example from my own life.

Lately I've been thinking a lot about breasts. My mother's breasts that I remember seeing and marveling at as we dressed and bathed together in the mornings. My daughter's newly formed breasts, which jiggle and bounce despite our best efforts to tame them with sports bras. My breasts, which my husband says in good humor are migrating south. The breasts of a woman whom I met early last year in Chicago who told me the story of her double mastectomy. Chicken breasts, which I loathe because I'm a dark meat woman. The breasts underneath the bulletproof vest that I worry my policewoman cousin Gail in Atlanta will forget to wear one day when she goes to lock up some criminal. I've been thinking a lot about breasts. I worry that my breasts are trying to tell me something. I am conscientious these days about giving myself breast exams. As important as these exams are for women my age, I have a feeling that prompting me to be more vigilant about giving myself breast exams is not all God has in mind. But what could it be?

Like many girls, the black-skinned Shulammite maiden in Song of Solomon grew up the target of jokes and taunts. Boys learn early of the message in our culture that girls' bodies are somehow mysterious and different from their own, and that the way to protect themselves from the mysteries of the female body is to learn how to ridicule and subdue it for their pleasure. What they don't understand when they're boys, they poke fun at. God help the sister or the girl at school who shows any sign of sensitivity about her body. I was always a head taller than every boy in my class, and I sprouted breasts at age nine as proof that I was different and more mature. I remember many afternoons sitting in class pretending not to notice or care about the drawings and jokes being passed around class about my spectacular "headlights." Even now as I sit here typing this forty-year-old story onto my computer screen, I can still feel a pinch of shame and wounded pride rising to the surface. I thought I was over that.

When you're a girl, the comments of family, friends, and enemies about the rapid or the glacial changes in your body can leave you in a puddle of tears. The Shulammite complains in the book's opening of being made to work outdoors in the sun, presumably during the hottest time of the day. And when they weren't forcing her to work out in the sun, her brothers were teasing her. They taunted her about her itty-bitty breasts (8:8). They fretted out loud that their sister's tiny (or no) breasts were sure to be a source of disappointment to a suitor who may one day come around to barter for her hand in marriage. The logic was: The bigger the breasts, the larger the bride-price a suitor would be willing to pay a maiden's family for her hand in marriage. Little bitty breasts spelled a little bitty bride-price. But they didn't stop there. They concocted ways to detract a suitor's attention away from their sister's flat chest. They imagined decking her in layers of elaborate silver necklaces, or layers of stiff hard clothing (8:9) to camouflage their sister's lack of breasts. There's no reason to doubt that the Shulammite's brothers loved their sister dearly. But brothers are notoriously strange creatures as every girl who has ever had one knows from experience. Instead of showering them with gifts and compliments, brothers express their love to their sisters by taunting them, belittling them, poking fun at their insecurities and driving them mad with their endless pranks. God save us.

The feisty maiden never gives her brothers (nor us) the pleasure of coming apart. Like the quick-witted maiden she is, she has her own comeback to hurl at them when they complain about her breasts. *My body is fine the way that it is, thank you.* (Spoken like a true gutsy girl on a playground. I wish I'd said as much when I was younger instead of sitting there pretending not to notice the notes being passed all around me.) "I [am] a wall, and my breasts [are] like towers" (8:10). She refuses to let her brothers tell her who she is. She is who she says she is. *I am invincible (to your definitions, anyway), and I am at peace with my breasts just the way they are.*

My, how much the world has changed in some respects, and how little it has changed in others! We are expected to share the brothers' prejudice against women with small breasts! We'd like to think as readers that we've come a long way since these words were written in the fifth century BCE. But we haven't. Not really. The millions of dollars women spend every year on breast enhancement surgery is proof that breasts continue centuries later to capture the sexual imagination. Women are raised to hate their bodies. I don't know a woman who doesn't wish she could change something about her body. What don't you like about your body? All of us can readily find something about our bodies we wish we could alter. Not because there really is anything inherently wrong with our thick lips, or kinky hair, or skinny legs, or curvy, curvy hips, or hairy upper lip, or unruly hairy eyebrows, or itty-bitty breasts. We've been taught to believe something is wrong with us the way we are. After all, the average girl is bombarded with scores of advertisements per week, and by the time she is seventeen years old, she has received over many thousands of commercial messages through the media. In the bulk of these advertisements the emphasis is on thinness as a standard for female beauty, and the bodies idealized are frequently atypical of normal, healthy women. In fact, today's fashion models weigh 23% less than the average female, and a young woman between the ages of eighteen and thirty-four has a 7% chance of being as slim as a catwalk model and a 1% chance of being as thin as a supermodel. This constant exposure to advertisements aimed at girls and women has the effect of making us self-conscious about our bodies and obsessive about our physical appearance as a measure of our worth. No wonder we grow up feeling unhappy with our bodies. Until, that is, we become sick and frail. That's when we wish we had taken better care of ourselves and loved sooner our bodies as they were. It wasn't until my friend Jamie was diagnosed with multiple sclerosis, an autoimmune disease of the central nervous system, that she begin to notice just how strong, well built, and reliable her legs (which she'd previously hidden under pants because they were impossibly hairy) had been all her life. An unexpected diagnosis can remind you that misshapen breasts are better than no breasts at all, and a head full of luxuriously kinky hair is much preferred to no hair at all. The Shulammite is content with her breasts as they are. She refuses to buy into the stereotype of the small-breasted woman as inferior and inconsequential. She refuses to absorb her brothers' unkind remarks. Carrying around the wounds they meant to inflict would only cause her more suffering in the end.

Since when did we allow our breasts, which are the symbol of our nurturing and life-enhancing powers, to be used against us? Our breasts were meant as a symbol of our ability to love and care as women. Our breasts were never meant to symbolize our willingness to give ourselves away to others for their pleasure and satisfaction. Breasts are the part of the female anatomy most identified with nurturing. They are also the most highly charged area of our body, shamelessly exploited by our culture as somehow God's gift to men for the sole purpose of their erotic pleasure. But breasts are both literally and symbolically a symbol of nurturance in our society. Prolactin, the chemical that is activated after a woman gives birth, keeps the breasts full of milk and also enhances the process of the mother-child bonding through breast-feeding. Both milk and love flow to the child as a mother nourishes her child through her breasts. Prolactin has such a powerful effect that many women experience the "letdown" reflex, which fills the breasts with milk, the moment they hear their infant crying. Small wonder when we turn to the Bible that one of the names for God is El Shaddai. The Hebrew word *shad* is used twenty-four times in the Old Testament and is most often translated as "breast." Therefore, in the same way that a mother's breast is "all-sufficient" for her newborn's nourishment, God is "all-sufficient" for God's people. Hence, when we combine El (Almighty God) with Shaddai (All-Sufficiency), we have "The Almighty God who pours out sustenance and blessing." (Come on. You didn't really expect the all male committee responsible for translating the Hebrew to English to translate literally as "The Almighty (Big) Breasted God," did you?)

What are my dreams and thoughts about breasts trying to tell me? Can the fact that I dreamed about my mother's breasts the other night mean nothing more than I was exhausted when I fell into bed, and the last thing on my mind was the mammogram I had scheduled the next day? Can the little sharp pains coursing through my breasts be the result of the normal monthly changes in my hormone levels? Or could they also be messages my body is trying to send me that I'm carrying too much, doing too much, under too much stress, worrying about too much? Who am I holding too close? Who (and what) am I nursing that I should be weaning off me? What (or who) am I holding on to and refusing to let go?

"Renita, the lump is malignant." Claudette's words over the telephone that December evening sent me crumbling into the chair. "The doctor says it's cancer," she said.

I can still taste the fear that accompanied her diagnosis. It was my turn to speak, but I didn't trust the scream welling up inside to fully articulate my horror. Incoherent words swirled through my head: "My girlfriend has breast cancer." The words did not sound right. They did not fit together. They made no sense to me. "My girlfriend is too young to have breast cancer; I am too young to know someone with breast cancer. She is my girlfriend. Friends don't get cancer."

I wrote those words more than twelve years ago. I have learned a lot about breast cancer since then. Girlfriends do get cancer. Young and old women get breast cancer. Black women are more likely, however, to die from breast cancer because we're less likely to get medical attention when the cancer is still at a treatable stage. By the time we show up in doctors' offices, the cancer is usually at a more advanced stage. In other words, we put off examining our breasts. We spend ourselves nurturing other people's wounds and dreams, and neglect our own. Whether we're twenty-five, forty-five, or sixty-five, we are lax about self-care and lack any vigilance about doing what we should to preserve our emotional, physical, and spiritual health.

They say that the best treatment for breast cancer is early detection. But early detection requires routine self-examination. And for a woman to examine her breasts, she must admit that she has them. How do you teach a woman to examine and protect a body that she doesn't see as her own? How can she take responsibility for her health when the messages from billboards, pop music, commercials, and religion are that she is property for other people's pleasures, fantasies, and rages? Good health is a correlate of healthy self-esteem. Assassinate a woman's ego, kidnap her spirit, take away her appetite for living, and you don't have to worry about her body. She will kill herself with food, delayed medical attention, and codependent, addictive relationships.

Some doctors point to scientific studies that draw a correlation between emotional style and the incidence of breast cancer, and a woman's ability to recover from breast cancer. Severe crises such as divorce, death of a loved one, or loss of a job within five years preceding detection of a suspicious breast lump increase the chance of the lump being cancerous. According to the studies, those women who did not allow themselves to grieve fully the losses they experienced were three times likely to suffer from breast cancer. This news makes me anxious to get at the source of my own preoccupation lately with breasts. If we are indeed in essence spiritual beings having a physical experience, I know intuitively that part of what my fixation with breasts is trying to tell me is that I need to take better care of myself. I also need to notice that I haven't been doing my part to create more mutually reinforcing relationships in my life. I keep getting myself in relationships that suck the life out of me. I see one coming, but I don't do anything about it until it's too late.

The dark-skinned Shulammite teaches us that we have to insist upon our right to feel and love fully, and our right to protect ourselves from people who sneak into our lives and take advantage of our love. Although there will be moments in life when we'll be tempted to stuff our feelings inside, deny what we're feeling, ignore what we're feeling for the sake of seeming strong for those around us, the Shulammite teaches us through her poetry the importance of being able to express joy, love, grief, and forgiveness, as well as anger and hostility. We mustn't allow ourselves to be made ashamed of our emotions. When a woman's emotions are blocked, her health is jeopardized. The Shulammite is in love with the mysterious shepherd, who flits in and out of sight during the verses of the book. But she doesn't allow love to make her blind to her own self-esteem and self-worth. Her breasts, whether they are large, small, or nonexistent, are hers. They are evidence of her ability to form loving relationships that nurture and sustain. After all, she is the daughter of El Shaddai, the God who knows personally and viscerally the importance of being able to bond with those you love, grieve over those things that will never be, and forgive those who refuse your love.

Reflections on Your Body

❦

Women are raised to hate their bodies. I don't know a woman who doesn't wish she could change something about her body. What don't you like about your body?

1. What about your body do you wish you could change?

_____

_____

_____

2. What health conditions are common among the women in your family? When was your last physical exam? Pap smear? Breast exam?

_____

_____

_____

3. What signals does your body send to let you know when you're tired and need to rest? When you're stressed? Sick? In over your head?

_____

_____

_____

4. What has your body been trying to tell you lately?

_____

_____

_____

5. When you think of growing old, who best models the kind of the woman you wish to be like most as you grow older. Why?

_____

_____

_____

6. Meditate on the words to this well-known psalm (Psalm 139): *I praise you, for I am fearfully and wonderfully made. Wonderful are your works, and my soul knows it very well.* Write a poem of praise and thanksgiving for your body—the one you were born with.

_____

_____

_____

Sacrifice

"Put simply, love costs."

Your desire for a full and fulfilling life will necessitate your learning that following your desires does not mean following every whim, nor indulging your pleasures to excess, but accepting that life and sacrifice go together. If you want to live debt free, you will have to stop impulsive buying. If you want to go back to school, you will have to sacrifice money and time. If you want to rise to the top in your career, you will have to devote long hours to work and be prepared to postpone starting a family. If you marry this man, you will have to give up wondering whether the other one might have made a better husband. If you wish to commune deeper with God, you will have to devote yourself to periods of meditation when the goal is to empty yourself of turmoil. I'm talking here about more than making choices. I'm talking about deferring gratification, that is, learning to discipline your desires, postponing some pleasures, and harnessing your passion for the sake of larger goals or purposes in mind.

Our belief in instant satisfaction is the curse of our age. In a society with an addiction to excess like ours, we may be tempted to close our ears to this chapter. Why must we learn to control our desires? After all, passion isn't passion unless it makes you feel out of control and unable to resist. But that's precisely the reason why you ought to proceed with caution. Passion isn't a bad thing in itself, but its power to consume you with such a thrilling, yet aching sense of yearning that causes everything else in sight to blur in comparison is why you ought to be careful about stirring up such an energy force.

To give yourself over to passion is to lose all sense about yourself, and to almost lose your mind, at least for a while. Things return to normal eventually, thank God, but not before everything and everyone else dear are almost lost to you for want of attention. Put simply, there are times in your life when being distracted by desire may be too costly. The mature woman knows that there are some seasons when you have to postpone all that achy-breaky yearning until a better time.

What a slap in the face you're probably thinking right about now. What hypocrisy. What an about-face for the Shulammite to make. Now that she's convinced us to trust our desires as women, to not allow our dreams and passions to be hemmed in by our culture, how can she turn around and try to clamp down on the tidal wave that she's unleashed. Particularly as women, we've been made to feel guilty for wanting anything for ourselves other than to take care of others. It feels like a backlash to ask us now to sacrifice pleasure. Self-denial has been our lot for centuries. But that's the point. Don't be fooled into thinking that you can make up for a lifetime of denial and sublimation through excesses of pleasure, passion, or even rage. You will quickly discover that starvation will make you prone to accept any substitute offered.

In fact, when you allow yourself to run amok chasing every opportunity to binge on your wildest desires, three things are likely to happen to you. First, you run the risk of losing your ability to sense danger when it's near. Your instincts become dulled by the bingeing, and you aren't able to notice territory violations when they happen. Second, you're likely to start making excuses for violating some of your own rules that you hold dear. That's when internal hemorrhaging sets in, where you pretend that everything's cool when internally it's not, but you can't bring yourself to say anything that might end the fantasy. And third, you know you're in minimum subsistence mode when you're unable to intervene on your own behalf to say enough is enough. When deterioration happens, the only way out is to relearn the deep lessons of bringing your desires into balance.

Have you ever noticed that some women find it easier than others to fall in love? I have. It's part of their makeup. Love is never as complicated for some women as it is for the rest of us, or so it seems. With each love affair, my friend Delores is more convinced than before that she has found the perfect sweetheart. She goes through a series of intense romances, swept up by the magic of being in love. In fact, she is in love with being in love. She prefers courtship to commitment and roses to the real nuts and bolts of building a relationship. In the magic of each moment, she insists that she has met the man of her dreams, who is like a god. But she soon discovers what you and I already know, that you can't toil away day in and day out in the pinch and pull of a relationship slugging it out with a god for a lover. Men who are gods make lousy partners. But adolescent-like women such as Delores refuse to accept this fact. Rather than accept the men they attach themselves to as humans with warts and all, which is the only way to grow in romance, they drop their lovers whenever they show signs of having clay feet. They replace them with others more perfect, more godlike, more elusive and fictional. But this kind of love can only make a woman "sick" (5:8). Exhausted. Self-destructive. Ravaged. She has worked against her own best interests. (Besides, not all lovers are that easy to dump.) The maiden cautions us all about the dangers of leaping into love every chance you get. Passion can be frightening, even dizzying, catching us off balance. Reason vanishes. Your defenses are down. Before it's done with you, passion will see to it that you're a loser as many times as you're a winner. That's because love costs. You catch yourself saying and doing, surrendering and acquiescing to, things you never thought possible.

Mysticism has long emphasized the importance of learning how and when to call in your senses. Too much indulgence has a dizzying, overwhelming effect. Here's where overindulgence becomes a distortion of freedom. *"Your love is like wine,"* the Shulammite confessed to her lover (1:2). Love can make you take leave of your senses. Drink to your heart's content and you're likely to wind up numb to pain and to pleasure. One way to call in your senses is by spending time refocusing your energies in ways that lead to emptying yourself of every thought and impulse that keeps you stirred up, agitated, and distracted. The need to have the last word. That craving for sweets. Your devotion to a favorite sitcom. An obsession with shopping. The whole point of meditation is not fasting, vigils, or flagellation. Rather, it's a matter of emptying the mind of distractions, turmoil, or anything that competes with the soul's ultimate desire, namely to make contact with something larger than one's own ego. So, too, sometimes there are seasons when we need to be free from our desires, to step back and get some perspective on them, in order for us to be able to appreciate and recognize the forces that have been working all along on our behalf to help us and to undo us.

We are masters at avoiding a confrontation with the real person that we are, which is why this is hard work. We can play games, put on masks, go off on tangents, lose ourselves in fantasies, even busy ourselves with acts of religiosity to avoid the real silence in which we look at our inner feelings. To an outsider, the sacrifices the person who is intent on refocusing her energies makes seem painful. Heading off to a monastery for a week's retreat instead of to one's time-share in Vail. Sitting still and quiet for hours on end in meditation. Refusing meat during the Lenten season. Shaving your head bald. Taking a vow of celibacy. To the outsider, these feel like painful measures to take, but the outsider hasn't caught the vision of something that is invisible to the outsider, something indescribably desirable to the insider. The outsider sees only what's being sacrificed. The insider sees what's to be gained. Detachment. Focus. Simplicity. Realignment. Jesus said it best perhaps: ". . . unless a grain of wheat falls into the earth and dies, it remains just a single grain; but if it dies, it bears much fruit." (John 12:24) Only in surrendering ourselves to something greater than our desires are we able to gain ourselves back. Only by abandoning self does one achieve self-realization. Sacrificing temporary pleasures in the hopes of pursuing a more lasting, more desirable pleasure is the ultimate goal of the spiritual journey, isn't it?

The Shulammite is not turning around and bad-mouthing pleasure and desire. She simply warns the daughters of Jerusalem, and us all, to keep desire in its perspective. There's nothing wrong with sexual passion, but remember that sexual passion doesn't go far enough. Once the ecstasy passes, you're left numb and agitated, hungry for the next wave of passion to stir you to life again. It's pretty apparent that our heroine isn't wary of love and passion; she has just learned the limitations of lust. The desire to obliterate the distance between you and the object of your love, to entangle your bodies in the clutches of climatic delight, is understandable. But we are more than a body. Relationships based solely on physical attraction cannot survive. The body's search for union with another is symbolic of the soul's search for oneness with God. Be careful that that search for God does not take a backseat once the libido is aroused.

Timing is everything, says the Shulammite, agreeing with the writer of Ecclesiastes. Everything has its appropriate season. Even lust and love. Notice that the lovestruck heroine who earlier in the poetry is lightheaded with passion becomes by 2:7 the worldly woman and savvy teacher. Her roller-coaster ride with romance has made her a teacher of wisdom. The book itself is one of several in the Old Testament that scholars associate with Israel's ancient wisdom tradition with its emphasis on practical knowledge (Proverbs), its contemplation on the limitations of human reasoning (Jobs, Ecclesiastes), and its reflection on the power of human desire (Song of Solomon). Like her male counterpart in Ecclesiastes, the Shulammite is impatient with conventional wisdom (though she is less pessimistic about life than her counterpart) and sets her mind to explore the power and limitations of love.

Three times the wizened heroine admonishes the Jerusalem daughters to proceed with caution in matters of the heart (2:7; 3:5; 8:4). Like a good teacher, she wants to pass along to others what she has learned. The Hebrew meaning of the verb for *adjure* is "to swear solemnly." Together with the reference to the gazelles and does of the field, what we have here is probably a formulaic expression equal to the way we plead to be listened to: "I beg you with everything in me." Three times in the book she pleads with the Jerusalem daughters to weigh love.

I adjure you, O daughters of Jerusalem,
by the gazelles and the hinds of the field;
do not arouse love or awaken love
until it is ready.

The Shulammite sounds like a mother of a teenage daughter. How do you reason with a teenager who's in the throes of her first infatuation? You watch with joy and terror as she blossoms under its spell. You remember, but you try not to impose your memories upon her. You try warning her to go slow. You try reasoning with her not to lose sight of everything you've taught her: "Don't let your body write a check that your soul can't cash." You watch her preen and giggle when her new beau comes around. Everything you say is at odds with what she's feeling. "I beg you, sweetheart, with everything in me not to do anything foolish." You try talking with her about what's she's feeling. But love has cast its spell. She can't hear you, it seems. Finally, you threaten to kidnap her and lock her in her room for six months until the spell of love wears off. But your girlfriends talk you out of it and urge you to watch and pray instead, which is all a mother can do in most instances anyway. You pray a mother's prayer. "God, protect my child from herself. She has her whole life in front of her."

"Our love will be different," a seventeen-year-old daughter tells her distraught mother who's pleading with her daughter to take it slow in this new relationship. "Just because you and Dad didn't make it doesn't mean my relationship is doomed to failure." How do you begin to make her understand what you're trying to tell her?

She thinks you've never been in love. She thinks that you were born "suspicious and negative," that you don't know what it feels like to be unable to concentrate, eat, bathe, or breathe for being consumed with an achy longing that threatens to sear your flesh from your bones. The idea of her Neanderthal mom (grandmother or aunt) ever having been strung out on love is impossible for her teenage mind to imagine. Boy, would she be surprised to know the other you. How do you tell your daughter that her sensible mom is the same lovesick teenager who once called hundreds of times in one night, and hung up without saying a word, just to hear the voice of a pimply-faced boy who wore an Afro comb in his hair? But perhaps it's precisely stories like this that she needs to hear. Sometimes, it's not until we're able to strip naked as a bark on a tree that we become human, vulnerable, recognizable, in our children's eyes.

Three times the Shulammite reminds the Jerusalem daughters that timing makes all the difference in the world. Perhaps she repeats herself because she's lamenting her failure to follow her own advice. Perhaps she's trying to convince herself. Perhaps she is urging her audience. "Do what I say, not as I do." (She uses the formula one other place in the book, in 5:8, but there she's already a goner. Passion has gotten the best of her. "If you see my beloved, tell him that I am sick with love.") The Jerusalem daughters represent parts of herself, for sure, but her advice is wise and solemn enough to justify every woman giving heed. Sometimes a tale of private lust can make for a good public lecture on caution, restraint, and patience.

But exactly what does our heroine mean by warning us not to stir up or awaken love "until it's time?" Put simply, love costs. It often exacts a high price from those who fall prey to it. To fall in love, as frightening as this may sound, is to surrender your autonomy and your sense of self-control. The intense focus on each other is consuming. Can you afford to lose it? Do you have the fare for the ticket? Is the time right for the storminess of romance? Is this a good time to be torn into pieces by the pull and tug of intimacy? But there is never a good time for love if we follow this line of reasoning, you're probably thinking. The Shulammite agrees. That's her point. The time is never right to fall in love, but some times are worse than others. There are times when your career goals take precedence over a marriage proposal. There are times as a single mother when after a stormy, messy divorce your kids' welfare and sense of stability ought to matter more to you than the chance to date the handsome new guy on the job. And don't be surprised if a prospect for romance comes along just about the time you set your mind to devoting yourself to a spiritual retreat with God for the next six months. Sometimes love's timing is off, plain and simple. You meet the right person at the wrong time. Other goals can make it impossible to leap at love whenever it presents itself, the Shulammite reminds us. She's not trying to sound a note of defeat or resignation about life and love, like, say, the writer of Ecclesiastes. We're not condemned to living dry, dusty lives empty of passion and desire. She insists simply that we all have the responsibility to make an effort to pace ourselves and tame our desires, lest they cause us to do something utterly foolish and wind up bankrupting our future.

Finally, the Shulammite's warning to the Jerusalem daughters throughout Song of Solomon reminds us that love takes time. It takes time to see people for who they really are instead of the gods we invented in our minds. Our feisty, headstrong maiden isn't telling you and me anything we don't know already. But it's difficult to hear her warning when you're in the throes of a new romance. Who wants to hear, "Slow down, what you're looking for quite possibly can't be found?" It goes against everything you're feeling right at the moment. This feels so real, so urgent, so right. But that's precisely why we need the Shulammite's caution to help us maneuver through the light-headed world of love and romance. "Slow down. Don't lose your head," she warns women. "Don't lose your *self* because you're likely to need her one day." The Shulammite is the voice of our mothers pleading with us on our cell phones. She's your grandmother waiting up for you when you stumble into the house late at night dizzy from all the petting that just took place. She's your godmother who says she is taking you on a shopping spree but whose real aim is to get you to talk about the passion mark on your neck. She's my girlfriend who phones me in the middle of writing this chapter screaming that she suspects her seventeen-year-old daughter is pregnant and "Why would she do this when she saw firsthand how difficult life was for me trying to raise her as a single mom?" She's the English school-teacher who told you you had a gift for poetry and handed you a book of poems by Nikki Giovanni to study, but who began to show signs of worry when she stumbled upon you at your locker giggling and looking eagerly in the eyes of the boy with a ring in his ear and some expletive tattooed across his knuckles.

Who wants to hear that what you're feeling right now is probably lust and not love. Who cares? Who wants to hear that it takes time to find true love? You must find it in yourself before you can recognize it in someone else. But the Shulammite knows that this is precisely what we need to hear. She's the voice of God urging us, pleading with us, cautioning us not to abandon our first *real* love, our desire to live a full and fulfilling life based on those things dear to us.

Reflections on Sacrifice

Who wants to hear the words, "Slow down, don't lose your head"? It goes against everything you're feeling right at the moment. This feels so real, so urgent, so right. But that's precisely why we need the Shulammite's caution to help us maneuver through the heady world of love and romance. "Don't lose your *self*", she warns women, "because you're likely to need her one day." You would do well to heed the Shulammite's warning.

1. The next time this happens: _____

_____

I will know it's the Spirit warning me to slow down and pray before leaping.

2. How do you know when you're in love? When was the last time you felt that "thrilling, yet aching sense of yearning so strong that it causes everything else in sight to blur in comparison" sort of love?

_____

_____

_____

3. If love brings such joy, why does it tend also to bring so much pain?

_____

_____

_____

4. How do you know when you've fallen in love? What kind of woman are you when you're in the throes of love?

_____

_____

_____

5. In what ways is the spiritual journey similar to the journey of falling and being in love with another human being? What does love teach us about God and the cycle of life?

_____

_____

_____

Sex and Love

"Since when did smart women begin admitting that they have problems finding love?"

Your desire for a full and fulfilling life may include finding a lifelong partner, and if it does, it will help a lot if you have a pretty clear idea in your head and heart what you are looking for in a mate. Disregard what the naysayers say about the unlikelihood of a wise, daring, emotionally and spiritually healthy woman like yourself finding love. Even though all around us our culture mocks our quest for love saying that the number of eligible mates for us to choose from is small, that we're too smart and accomplished for our own good, that we're too old to be considered desirable, that what we're asking for from potential partners is unreasonable, never give up on your hope of finding love. It's easier to cave in to the stereotypes and pretend you're not the woman you've struggled to become; it's easier to eroticize submission as a not-so-bad price to pay for the illusion of being loved; it's easier to accept lust and sex as substitutes for love and communion than it is to hold out for what your heart and soul need in a relationship. But don't. Eventually the bill for lying to yourself for all these years comes due. You wake up one morning crazed with longing. A cord snaps inside, and everything in you cries out for something more: wholeness, depth, communion, freedom, genuine intimacy, and a peace within. And no one, not even you, understands where it will all end.

Throughout *What Matters Most*, I've tried to identify our spiritual nodal points, crucial points of intersection that align themselves and call for us to choose, face, dare, risk, decide. They are those pivotal moments of decision making that alter your future. Decisions about love, life, family, work alter *you* permanently. You set goals for yourself. You tell yourself that, come what may, you'll always remain true to yourself. You work hard at self-exploration and self-development. The lessons of self, identity, truth, balance, choices, inner wisdom, danger, the body, and sacrifice are ones you embrace without flinching. But then comes one that touches you at the core. You embrace its lessons, perhaps, but not without feeling as though you've given up so much already, this time you feel as though you're being asked to strip to the bark. After all, woman cannot live on self-love alone. It's the lesson of sex and love. Putting it off makes the bill only more costly when it comes due.

Let's face it: There are moments in your life when you have to decide how long you're going to permit sex, and the illusion of a relationship, to be a substitute for genuine love. I'm not talking here about choosing between sex and love. The two were meant from the beginning of God's creation to go hand in hand. But they don't, not always. You wake up one day and realize that you've spent your life spilling your life energy (your passion) on men who desired you enough to seduce you into letting down your mask and opening yourself up to them, but didn't love you enough to stay around to pick up the pieces when life came crashing down on you. Great sex with men who are relationship terrorists, men who seduce you by giving you enough of what you long for to gain your trust only to abruptly withhold it once you let down your guard, costs you.

We dreamed so long of being rescued and swept away by passion that we never noticed that sexual passion is not to be confused with true love. We can't help ourselves. It has to do with the script we've been fed since girlhood—a script that has been reinforced throughout our adult lives. *Cinderella. Sleeping Beauty. Waiting to Exhale. Pretty Woman. The Bridges of Madison County. Sex and the City.* We are drawn to juicy romance novels, soap operas, celebrity love affairs, and crooning love lyrics. We like to believe that passion means the abandonment of reason in the reckless pursuit of bliss. Rushing off to the Bahamas with some steroid-enhanced physical trainer who drives a Lexus, instead of showing up for choir rehearsal to rehearse the part you're supposed to sing in the cantata. Now that's passion. Bring us wine and roses, and we will faint with sensation, run naked with wolves, make out in the mail room, act out our X-rated fantasies, and forget to pick up our children after school. Men, by contrast, are the exact opposite, the script warns. Lust may make men abandon reason and risk everything to make out in the Oval Office. But when it comes to passion—well, let's just say that passion is what the other sex reserves for sports, careers, and cars.

The Shulammite's poetic yearnings in Song of Solomon permit us to step back from our own inchoate experiences with passion and romance to study the fantasies of an ancient woman, and we eagerly comb through her story to test whether her fantasies ring true to our own experiences of longing and desire. But our curiosity goes further. What's to be gained from eavesdropping on a nameless, dark, heartsick woman who is in the throes of passion? How did her salacious speech make its way into Holy Writ, you're probably wondering by now. After all, the Bible concerns itself with somber themes such as faith, prayer, hope, joy, salvation, eternity, the spirit, God, and the like. Sex, sexuality, sensuality, romance, and the erotic are the stuff of those mired in the messiness of mortality. Spirituality is supposed to take your mind off the flesh's desires. Only religious passion, the sort that subdues the flames of the carnal flesh (the body) and ignites an all-consuming longing to please God, is the stuff of pious contemplation. But the woman who speaks up in Song of Solomon evidently thought otherwise. Her book of poetry reminds us that sex and sexuality are as old as creation itself. Being sexual is, in fact, part of being human, and a very important aspect of our humanity. Her poetry bestows on us sacred lessons from which we can all learn as we practice the art of distinguishing between love that gives and lust that takes away.

Throughout all our lives, whether male or female, we long for and search after relationships that promise genuine intimacy, relationships that will touch the core of our innermost being. We are eager to find people, that someone, with whom we can be ourselves, expose who we are, relax, and just be. We're like the Shulammite, who risks life and limb to go after the love of our dreams.

> *Throughout the night as I lay in bed*
> *I yearned for him whom my heart loves.*
> *I sought him, but did not find him.*
> *Let me hasten to go about the city,*
> *through its streets and squares;*
> *and search for the one my heart loves.*
> *Let me look for him even if I don't find him.*
>
> (3:1–2)

Like lots of women you trust that your heart at the right moment will tell you when you will meet Mr. Right and convince yourself that a bell will sound within and you'll know that special someone when he comes along. That sort of answer plays out well on the big screen, if you like romantic comedies. But it's unwise to bank on romance sneaking up on you as it does for Meg Ryan in *When Harry Met Sally, Sleepless in Seattle,* and *You've Got Mail.* That way, I suppose, you can blame it on your heart, on fate, on God, when Mr. Goodbar turns out to be Mr. Goodfornothing. "How did you manage to fall for such a creep?" your best friend asks you over lunch as you pour out the latest relationship horror tale. "It just happened," you answer, feeling exonerated. That's a logical explanation for your failure to make better romantic choices. Isn't it? Weren't we raised to believe that love isn't love if it doesn't make mush of your brain?

If you were a teenager like me, reading piles of romantic pulp fiction under your bedcovers with a flashlight (*True Confessions*, *True Love*, *True Romance*, and *True Story*) and had megadoses of romantic fantasies designed to keep you in a state of prolonged adolescence, then like me, you're probably a sucker for a love story that depicts two unsuspecting people stumbling on to each other and falling headlong in love. Have you ever noticed that sometimes it's just the thought of falling in love, the sensation of losing control and taking leave of your senses, that some women long for? That's far more romantic than *being* in a relationship and having to negotiate the waxing and waning of intimacy. "I love being married," the female caller tells the radio talk show host. "I just miss being in love." Ah yes, falling in love: Who can resist the heady rush of falling headlong over a cliff with nothing more than a bungee cord around your ankle? And just think: Someone else feels the same way about you. Who can resist the seductions of a man hell-bent upon sweeping you off your feet with his advances? Can you believe it? How did Mark Twain put it? Oh yeah . . . "Love: The irresistible desire to be irresistibly desired."

The hardest lesson to get through to many of the young women I meet and speak with on college campuses (who themselves have been brought up on mega-doses of romantic pulp) is that not every man is worthy of you just because he falls in love with you. "When you don't stand for anything, you'll fall for anything," my stepmother would caution me when I answered "I don't know" to her questions about what I liked about this person or that person whom I'd chosen as a friend. But women older than the college students I teach can be just as eager to throw caution to the wind for that word-less rush that comes with romantic desire. It saddens me to have to admit that when asked what they are looking for in a relationship, even some of my high-achieving friends can't answer with anything approximating clarity.

When asked what three characteristics they are looking for most in a partner, most women are likely to say, if they are under thirty, "Strong, good-looking, and rich." If they are between thirty and forty, they may say, "Strong, communicative, and employed." If they are over forty, they're apt to say something along the lines of "strong, intelligent, and responsible." Age brings about lots of changes in what women want in partners. But being a strong man is one characteristic that never fails to make the list. Women insist that they want men who are strong. But what do we mean when we say we want strong men? "Take charge, but not too take charge," says a woman friend I asked. "Dominating without being domineering," said another. "Self-assured, but not arro-gant," quipped another. We are raised to believe that love isn't love, and a man isn't a man, unless he/it sweeps you off your feet, unless he overpowers you and leaves you feeling weak, out of control, breathless, unable to think clearly. It's not surprising to hear women of faith describe their ideal mate as someone who's both tough and sensitive, hard and gentle, powerful and compassionate. Is it really possible to be both these things at the same time? Is it unfair to ask men to be both? We say that we'd be willing to give up a tough, dominating, and self-assured man for a sensitive, gentle, compassionate one. But is that true? That's why I'm as convinced as ever that the love lyrics between the two sweethearts in Song of Solomon are a great springboard for getting women to talk about sex and power, and our confusion about the two.

I mentioned in the Introduction how Song of Solomon stands out in Christian Scripture because of the strong female imagery found in it and the fact that nowhere in its eight chapters is there any explicit mention of God. But what do we make of the fact that neither is there any explicit talk among the young lovers about consummating their passion within the bonds of marriage? Can you imagine: The hot and steamy love affair taking place before our eyes is between two people who are not yet married! Even though it remains unclear whether our heroine and her lover ever managed to turn their fantasies into reality by consummating their love, there's no denying that what we have in the Bible is two unmarried people groping, gawking, and fantasizing about what it must be like to explode in the embrace of one's desire. Sex: It's what young girls fantasize about and grown women consider their right. "How long am I supposed to wait?" young, single women ask just about the time they begin to suspect that getting married in their twenties (or thirties!) may not be a given. "What am I supposed to do about my needs?" those divorced, widowed, in sexually unsatisfying marriages, or single and over forty demand to know. Judging from the talk shows blasting across the airwaves, ours is a generation that believes having sex is an inalienable right and achieving an orgasm is an entitlement.

I know already that the fact that I'm happily married makes anything that I might say on the topic of sex outside marriage suspect. I don't bother telling folks that I was single for the first thirty-seven years of my life. I don't bother telling them that it took having sex inside a marriage relationship to teach me why there's so much hoopla in the Bible about sex outside of marriage. Sex is more than an act; it's a powerful force. It makes you think you feel things that you don't, and it keeps you from thinking about things that you would do well to think about.

It took making love within marriage for me to learn all that you're signing on to when you climb in bed with someone, twist and contort your body this way and that, slow down and speed up your breathing, grope at and stroke each other, exchanging fluids, all in the hopes of exploding in a fit of joyous pain with the other. More than body fluids are exchanged in moments like these. Why didn't anyone ever tell us flower children of the sixties, us make-love-not-war advocates of the seventies, that whole histories of life energy are being exchanged in that moment of sexual release? His history (physical, emotional, spiritual) becomes a part of your history. Your dreams get twisted and folded into his dreams. His neuroses become your neuroses. Your life energy gets genetically grafted onto his life energy. His demons become your demons. Perhaps that's what the writer of Genesis meant by "and the two shall become one" (Genesis 2:24). There are some lovers who remain indelibly encoded within your psyche, and you know it every time their names come up in conversation. The names and addresses of other lovers may be long forgotten, but somewhere within there is a vault that keeps a tally of where the bits and pieces of your self have gone. There are also bits and pieces of energy (both negative and positive) you've stored up from lovers past and gone stored away inside you. A shower can wash away his fluids from your thighs, but it can't easily wash away his scent from your life. A lover remains unexplainably, mysteriously, undeniably a part of you forever, even a casual lover, for better or for worse.

So what's so great about marriage? How about if I just answer what sex within a covenanted union was meant to be according to biblical thinking. The ideal of marriage is that it's supposed to offer you the protective covering to risk opening up and sharing your deepest secrets. Baring your emotional and psychic wounds, opening your soul, exposing your shadows, without fear that the other will shrink away from what he or she discovers. After all, your secrets are now becoming his secrets, and vice versa. His demons are now your demons. Your healing inspires his healing. His wholeness opens up a space for your wholeness. Perhaps this explans why the Bible frequently refers to sexual copulation as "knowing," as in "and [Abraham] *knew* [Sarah] . . ." To know someone and to be known by that same someone is to make yourselves vulnerable to each other's past, present, and future. No more masks. "Naked, and not ashamed" is another way the writer of Genesis put the matter. The expectation, since biblical times, was that you wouldn't want to trust the raw, exposed truth about who you are unmasked to someone who's not invested in helping you be the best you. What's more, it was believed that when lovers committed to each other merge their bodies together in the raw naked act of sexual intercourse, sex has the potential to become a vehicle (one among a number, I suppose) through which male and female in the mystical union of coupling experience the sacred, witness the Divine, and even glimpse their own possibilities as spiritual beings. The ancients understood sex to be a spiritual act, a way to experience otherworldliness, which could be achieved only when male and female, which are incomplete without each other, come together in complementary fashion. That's why marriage is referred to as a *union*, a sacred union at that, the ultimate miracle, two flesh becoming one. I know. I know. It doesn't always happen that way. But it's a hell of an idea to aim for.

Which explains, perhaps, how the secular love poems of Song of Solomon eventually became a tract for talking about the human and divine love affair. The Shulammite's pining away for her elusive shepherd became akin to the Creator's desperate attempts to be known and revealed to his creation. And the shepherd's erratic pattern of pulling close and pushing away from the Shulammite maiden became a metaphor for human beings' own on-again, off-again love affair with the Sacred. In the mystical moment of consummation between two committed partners, whether occasioned by prayer or coupling, the past is forgotten, all trespasses are forgiven, life begins anew. That's what it's supposed to be like. I said before that it's an elusive goal. A utopian expectation. A far-fetched possibility. But there are those *seconds*, don't you remember, when you're in each other's arms, breathing in sync, lost in each other's touch, and swimming in each other's moisture when you've caught yourself being transported to . . . where? . . . another place? . . . another world? . . . another you? Mysterious is the way the mystics of the world put it. Unquenchable is the way the Shulammite describes it. It's the sort of experience of nakedness and relentless exploring of one's self that should not be trusted to a casual lover who has made no promises to you.

Throughout *What Matters Most*, I've tried to insist that Song of Solomon, despite what commentators say, is about more than sex. Sex is for most of us the drama around which we attempt desperately to capture our deepest desires, our most feverish longing, our recurring dreams, and our most aching loneliness. The Shulammite captures our imagination because throughout the book we recognize her desperate efforts to discover what it feels like to be loved, adored, cherished, beyond the moment of embrace. It's an experience many of us wonder about. What does it feel like to be loved? More important, if you're my age, what does it feel like to be loved for your mind and spirit, and not just for the suppleness of your body? What do you do as a woman when you're past the age when you can rely on your body to help you barter with your culture? It's a question the women I know wonder about a lot. They are the ones who have devoted their lives to trying to be well-rounded women—educated, accomplished, independent —who are at a crossroads as to what to do about the one thing that remains elusive and mysteriously absent from their portfolio: love. Is it too much to yearn for love that enhances rather than dominates, that stretches you instead of diminishes you, that inspires you to take risks rather than leaving you frightened and apologizing for your dreams?

"Since when did smart women begin admitting that they have problems finding love?" one of my students asked one day after a discussion of Song of Solomon. The truth of her words stung. A man who admits he is having problems finding the right love is highly evolved. A woman who admits the same is weak and pathetic. Her question sent me on a search for books by intellectual women who admit that, despite all their accomplishments, love remains one of the last unexplored frontiers. The pickings were slim, at least by authors who weren't admonishing women to cave in and settle for what they can get. But thank God there were a few. Intellectual women don't talk out loud often about how hard love is. It's certainly not something you write books about. Tax codes, Aramaic, postmodern philosophy, and the history of science we know. But who's willing to admit that most of us don't know a thing about what it takes to build a strong, healthy, committed relationship with the opposite sex? We are failures at the thing we crave most—love and intimacy. Marriage is no proof that you finally figured it out. If anything, it offers you proof positive that you're a failure. You find yourself locked daily in a battle with someone who reminds you that, with all your training and credentials, you don't have a clue about love and intimacy. Neither does he, mind you.

But the desire to experience satisfying love, and not just a banshee-screeching orgasm, is holy and noble work. Self-love may be the first order of business for any woman (or man) committed to personal growth and a healthy self. But you can't live on self-love alone. Loving and being loved by someone enhances your life. As difficult as marriage is, I'm better for having risked jumping the broom and throwing myself headlong into this cliff-hanger called marital union. Working monthly, daily, hourly, trying to build a loving union with my husband has added more to my life than it's taken from it. It's bloody, bruising, oftentimes humiliating work, the way it calls upon you to negotiate, compromise, roll with the punches, climb and hold on by your fingernails, explore and rediscover, and build and rebuild from scratch one Lego at a time a partnership that works for the two of you. But with the right person who's committed for the long haul (which in my case meant someone who was as gutsy and tenacious as I am), it can be good, holy work, the kind that transforms the soul for the better in the process.

Don't give up on finding love despite what the naysayers say. It's never too late to find true love. Instead of being made to feel weak and intellectually soft for admitting one's desire for love and its importance for one's well-being, the final lesson of the Shulammite is to not give up on your belief in the goodness of love and your inherent need to be loved. Even strong, independent-minded women need love. Don't settle for sex, even good sex. For even good sex has a way of blowing up in your face if it doesn't come with the promise of staying around and taking responsibility for the bill that comes due from a body that spent its youth indulging its sexual fantasies. Never give up on finding the love you yearn after. To do so is to give up on life itself. Finding love won't cure all your aches, nor will it protect you from the work of having to grow and learn to love yourself, and developing into the woman God created you to be. Not even true love can rescue you from yourself. But finding love can open up wonderfully new vistas for a woman committed to a life-time of personal growth and self-discovery. Despite all the ways the shepherd failed the Shulammite by pulling close and pushing away, by not staying around to see her through the things she learned about herself, eventually she would have to learn to thank him for what he offered, forgive him for what he wasn't capable of offering, and release him on to his own journey. You can't fight for something that was never there in the first place. Which is why it always makes sense never to give your vineyard completely away.

My vineyard, my very own, is for myself.

(8:12)

Your vineyard is where you keep your most valuable treasures—the people, memories, dreams, values, and lessons you've gathered over the years that contribute to making you who you are and that sustain you as you continue to grow. Part of that vineyard should always consist of the love that friends and family offer. Be intentional about surrounding yourself with people who can and do love you in nonsexual ways (that's whether you've found your soul mate or not). If you don't have *eros*—romantic, sexual love—in your life right now, cherish the *agape*— nonsexual relationships—that are in your life, made up of all the folks you know who cheer you on and are invested in what's best for you. Count yourself blessed for having carved out for yourself a circle of people who support you, protect you, encourage you, look after you, and will see about you when you can't see about yourself. That, too, is love. The body craves sex as an opening for intimacy, but the soul craves intimacy as a foundation for fulfilling sex and love.

Love that is embracing without being sexual is also good for the soul. Surrounding yourself with people, a community, a village whose love nourishes and supports you is just as essential. After all, it's love, connection, relationship, community, belonging that we're all seeking. Love that stimulates your heart to trust, believe, and keep hoping is love that keeps you alive and lends you an air of mystery. Lots of women can attest that it was only after they'd stopped settling for sex as a substitute for love, stopped stalking the streets groping for relationships in all the wrong places, that love sneaked up on them and found them. It's wonderful when love and all the lessons that come with living a full and conscious life find you early in life. But that probably isn't how it will happen for most of us. The amount of growing and evolving required to transform from being the hapless maiden in Chapter 1 of Song of Solomon to the self-possessed woman we witness in Chapter 8 most assuredly takes more than a few weeks. It takes years of shedding and growing, stumbling and starting again, before the young maiden of Chapter 1, who opens her poems blaming her brothers for her misfortune and missed chances, to metamorphose into the mature, evolved woman in Chapter 8, who reclaims her vineyard and takes responsibility for making herself happy.

But what about all the time that lapses between now and then? How can I keep from becoming impatient with myself? Is it possible to miss the lessons that knock at our door? Of course it is. The Shulammite was slow in answering the door in 5:2–6 and lost that chance to embrace her shepherd lover. It's certainly possible to miss lessons and to fail to grow. Sometimes we're not ready within when the invitation comes to choose wisely. If things are flashing by you, as you hurry here and there, trying to grab at everything you see, trying to stuff down your throat those things you fear are scarce and ephemeral, if you don't have time to examine your life and cherish where you are at this moment, you don't know that you don't know. You can't seize what you can't sense.

To be ready within is to be willing to trust God that there will be other opportunities to get it right. Next time you'll be ready. Sure, some opportunities come around once in a lifetime, but God is not like us. God gives us repeated chances to grow, change, and go to the next level. We miss some opportunities, for sure. We will miss this or that chance to declare who we are and what we want from life, but there will be other chances. We will ignore our better judgment and do some things counter to the lessons we've learned, but if we're lucky, we come out singed but not scorched and wiser next time. We will misjudge this person or that invitation and put ourselves in harm's way, but not next time. We will in a lifetime miss this or that chance at love because the timing was all wrong or the lover whose hand was extended out to us was only half present, but that will not be our only chance for love. There will be other chances. Other moments. Another intersection. "Behold I stand at the door and knock," says the Holy One. Be grateful that God is loving and committed enough to our becoming to knock repeatedly—until we're ready to open.

Reflections on Sex and Love

At the heart of *What Matters Most* is the statement found in this chapter, *Never give up on finding the love you yearn after. To do so is to give up on life itself. Finding love won't cure all your aches, nor will it protect you from the work of having to grow and learn to love yourself, and of developing into the woman God created you to be. Not even true love can rescue you from yourself.*

1. What characteristics about yourself matter most to you such that you are no longer willing to sacrifice them for the world's approval?

_____

_____

_____

2. What characteristics matter most to you in a potential mate?

_____

_____

_____

3. What lessons should we be passing on to our daughters, granddaughters, and goddaughters about love and sex?

_____

_____

_____

4. What was God's intention in creating sex?

_____

_____

_____

5. What do you now know at this stage in your life are the differences between lust and intimacy, sex and love? How has your understanding changed over the years?

_____

_____

_____

6. What is the positive principle God may be trying to teach you about who you are and where God wants to take you?

_____

_____

_____

Notes